The Public Church

Martin E. Marty

The PUBLIC CHURCH

Mainline-Evangelical-Catholic

CROSSROAD / NEW YORK

1981
The Crossroad Publishing Company
18 East 41st Street, New York, NY 10017

Printed in the United States of America

Library of Congress Cataloging in Publication Data

Marty, Martin E   1928–
   The public church.

   1.   Christianity—United States.   I.   Title.
BR526.M353   277.3   80-27120
ISBN 0-8245-0019-9

To the Reverend Arthur Simon
and the Honorable Paul Simon

Exemplars to three generations of Martys

Agents of the Public Church
in a world hungry for bread and justice and spirit

Contents

Preface

The North American churches have been suffering a crisis of morale and mission. The two aspects of the crisis connect. A dictionary defines morale as "the state of the spirits of a . . . group, as shown in willingness to perform assigned tasks, confidence, cheerfulness, and discipline." While millions of individuals and thousands of congregations are high-spirited performers, as movements their churches display demoralization.

The story of how this malaise feels and why it has grown for almost a generation in mainline Protestant and Roman Catholic churches is by now familiar. Serious leaders in evangelical Protestantism have also more recently begun to express dismay as their movement has been increasingly exposed to the acids of modernity. The widely advertised boom in conversions has not led to consistent and durable church growth. A new religious consumerism, they say, replaces a concern for the cost of discipleship. The market orientation of religion in the current revival leads it to cater to individuals but not to build community.

The Public Church is an address to this situation. Grounded in an historical understanding of the Christian churches in America, it draws on biblical, theological, and political motifs to offer a model for self-understanding and mission in the years ahead.

Part One details this model of a recently emerging ecumenical coalescence. The public church is seen as a "communion of communions" to match a political "community of communities" as a mode of organizing life.

The first chapter points to the largest scope of this complex, seeing it as a convergence of three large constituencies from within mainline Protestantism, evangelicalism, and Roman Catholicism. The second chapter, on the other hand, moves to the most intimate dimension as it traces the contribution of persons to the public church and its effect, in turn, on them. Mediating between the two are the congregations, the subject of chapter three, which suggests an urgent need for providing a fresh rationale in a world of privatism in religion.

Part Two has to do with various movements within the public church.

The first of these three chapters deals with the political character of a churchly complex in which not all elements agree or even are presumed to agree on everything. To mention politics is to imply compromise, which looks like a threat to prophetic integrity. This is an issue which demands attention. Then follows a reflection on ecumenism and evangelism, on unity and mission. Many today are encumbered by what they take to be a law of history: that only the belligerently exclusive grow, and that to be concerned with evangelism must mean to develop a kind of fanaticism that rules out other groups. Is this law true? Still another pair of motions or movements is implied in a third chapter on how private faith relates to the public order.

Part Three develops the sense of tensions when the public church encounters the public world.

The first of these chapters poses tribes versus tribalism, and shows how constituents of the church healthily provide a tribal sense but just as unhealthily can produce idols of tribalism. A corollary of this in the next chapter counterposes commitment and civility. This argument takes on another new law of history: that the civil must not be committed to any profound beliefs and that the committed dare not be civil toward others lest they lose their own faith. A final chapter in this section sets the enduring issue of drift or passivity over against churchly action. Instead of asking for a resuscitation of obsolete patterns of social action, these pages concentrate on ways in which, through congregational and personal life, Christians can be responsible in the public world.

I have written the book in a spirit of some urgency, motivated chiefly by two concerns. The first is the already mentioned listlessness in much of mainline Protestantism and Catholicism and of confusion in evangelicalism. On their present course these churchly movements could dwindle into relative insignificance, and we would see America without religious options beyond those that appeal to people in isolation from each other or that call for developing belligerent groups.

The second concern issues from a vision of the world near the end of the second millennium after Christ as a place where people huddle together over against each other and use religion to justify their over-againstnesses. The decline of civility has not reached crisis proportions in North America, but there is a disturbing decline of faith in the values of civility. I believe that what I am calling the public church has distinctive if not unique resources for exemplifying to a larger world a way of being faithful to the truth it knows, while showing "counter-intolerance" toward people with whom it disagrees and from whom it remains separate.

To call this a manifesto would be too grandiose and frantic; to think of it as a manual of arms is too militant. If it inspires in readers a response that leads them to say the equivalent of, "I never thought of it that way before," it might evoke creative disagreements and help produce patterns of actions that no single author or book can anticipate. In other words, I would like to think of it as being theoretical and practical at once.

While I hope that any reader can see that this argument is based in wide and deep research, the genre of the book is such that it did not seem to call for the kind of academic references appropriate in, say, a work of discovery in the discipline of history. Someone has said that a book dependent on one author is plagiarism, while one dependent on many shows research. This one is certainly dependent on many, but I have chosen to take the grist from such research and put it together in such a way that I have to take responsibility for the outcome.

Yet many people were of help along the way, not least of all the participants in seminars, lectureships, workshops, and the like. *The Public Church* grew out of six years' worth of such testings in literally hundreds of settings. Some of the ideas and references in the chapter on tribalism and civility appear in a very different context and form in my *By Way of Response* (Nashville: Abingdon Press, 1981). My assignment in that book was to give a kind of personal accounting of how I came to the positions that seem most important to me. This book is a setting forth of those positions. Therefore some overlap was inevitable. I do not think that readers of both books— may they be legion!—will feel cheated. I hope they will find the double angle of vision informing.

For the rest, I have resisted the habit of publishing individual lectures in book form, since the approach to ear and eye differs radically. Instead, it is my practice to accept research and speaking assignments which allow me to mull over a subject for years, to experiment with it and refine it in many kinds of audiences, be they religious or secular, academic or ecclesiastical in makeup. Then I transform what survives into a plotted essay.

Some who have heard these presentations in recent years may recognize here or there some familiar ideas, though I hope they will all be freshly stated in this essay. I cannot acknowledge all the hosts, but it would be ungrateful of me not to mention the sponsors of several endowed lectureships which provided the impetus and the opportunity for me to push thought in these directions. Among them are the hosts of the Merrick Lectures at Ohio Wesleyan University, the Snuggs Lectures at the University of Tulsa, the Shaffer Lectures at Northwestern University, the Fondren Lectures at Southern Methodist University, the Hayward Lectures at Acadia University, the Armstrong Lectures at Kalamazoo College, the Wickenden Lectures at Miami University, and the Wattson Lecture of the Friars of the Atonement at the Catholic University of America. If any of them wish to think of this book as in any way "theirs," that would be in order.

I dedicate it to a pair of brothers, a cleric and a congressman, who have been personal friends to my wife and me for a third of a century, who have been generous to our sons, and through inventions like *Bread for the World* and acts of legislation and works of love have embodied the style one looks for in any complex of churches that deserve the name "public"—or Christian.

Part One

A Communion
of Communions

1

The Three Constituencies

The public church is a family of apostolic churches with Jesus Christ at the center, churches which are especially sensitive to the *res publica*, the public order that surrounds and includes people of faith. The public church is a communion of communions, each of which lives its life partly in response to its separate tradition and partly to the calls for a common Christian vocation. In America the constituency of this convergence of churches comes from elements within the old mainline, the newer evangelicalism, and Catholicism. The public church does not await invention but discovery. When its participants recognize its scope, they can better realize their possibilities both individually and as a community.

The constituencies from the old "Protestant mainline"—a neologism referring to the long-established groups—have been most positively exposed to the culture. During their career they have known fewer difficulties than have others with the public order, but greater problems with being the church, with remaining intact as a center of loyalty to Christ. The newer evangelicals, who are moving on their separate track into the mainline, have had less problem with being the church in the sense of a called out and set apart body. But they have had more difficulties with public consciousness, with discerning how they are called to serve God also beyond their specialized field of saving souls out of the world. The Catholics have lived with charters that give them access as Catholics to the public sphere while retaining a coherent churchly existence. But not until a generation ago were they free formally to interact with other Christians to perform their tasks.

In 1975 Pope John Paul II, then still Karol Cardinal Woyjtyla of Cracow, authored a theological essay. One of its lines translates into a terse description of the two sides of the public church's life: *"The church possesses a special interiority and a specific openness."* The special interiority comes from its focus on Jesus Christ, the faith its members hold in common. This allows them communion with God and each other. It establishes a language of witness and worship. Interiority implies the movement of the gathered church as a body through time and in many places. By itself this aspect could lead to introversion and the church would become a company of people huddled together with their backs to the world.

The church, however, has also been gifted with a specific openness. This means that its worldly ties are mediated, focused, and disciplined. The church does not merely sprawl and spill itself until all its substance is gone. The relations to the world are selective; this church "picks its shots." But though tempered by this specificity, it *is* open. This means it is not only self-concerned with growth, resources, and interior life. Such an understanding of the church also animates whole church bodies outside Roman Catholicism and characterizes large elements within such bodies. Members of all these are now in position to recognize each other. A number of governing assumptions behind this book will begin to demonstrate why they should.

First, the reality of the secular order and disorder calls for alertness on the part of churches that are discriminatingly open. For several centuries as modern secularity unfolded in its startling ways, it appeared to be nothing but a threat to the churches. The secular horizon seemed devoid of promise for Christians. The skies were empty. Church bells still rang, but they did so under a canopy in which populations no longer expected a divine response from the heavens above. People seemed to have crossed a border that centuries before bounded their lives. They moved beyond the sacred, beyond the presence of a responsive God. So long as that concept of the secular held a monopoly, Christians had life easy. They could simply retreat into their specific interiority.

A generation or two ago, however, Christians asked what their callings might be within the secular order, which they now viewed more favorably as they received its gifts. God was active in the whole world, governing its encompassing life. The nations did not move beyond the care of the Lord of history. Christians were from the first to respond to the civil "powers that be" even when these were not congenial to the faith, because they *were* "ordained of God." For purposes of social truth or justice and in many other ways, people not moved by explicit faith were serving some revealed purposes of God. Was the church then free to shun their contributions?

In the act of recognizing secularity, however, some romantic zealots in the church, with overcompensating vigor, lost the sense of specific openness to it and they became merely open. In mainline Protestantism and to some extent in Catholicism some leaders almost lost the Christic center of the church in their eagerness to embrace the secular realm. Some of these secularizers endured as Christians. Within a few years many of them were observably more selective than they had been in dealing with the secular order.

During this period of reaction these Christians rediscovered the durability of the sacred and the marvellous staying power of religious impulses. This discernment led to some immediate underestimation of the secular, as if it had no reality of its own. Such an underestimation would seem on the face of it to be incredible to a thoughtful person who lives in the worlds of the higher academy, mass media of communication, literary and artistic culture, and commerce. Professor Langdon Gilkey has properly remarked that secularity is to moderns what Hellenism was to the Greeks; an envelope, a taken-for-granted aspect of reality. It will not die by a thousand qualifying definitions, nor will its assets and liabilities disappear tomorrow. The public church, because of its experience and its calling, is endeavoring to determine appropriate proper ways to live with secularity.

Second, the public church is gifted with its own understandings of religions outside the scope of biblical faith. The recent reactors against secularity were correct when they observed that religion had not disappeared. Modernity merely dislocated and relocated the sacred. The world religions survived and some of their sects prospered. Islam today is militant and expansive. Before the end of the second millennium, there will for the first time be more Christians in the southern than in the northern hemispheres. Buddhism and Hinduism have suffered setbacks but they also have taken on new life in aggressive revival movements. The totalitarianisms of the century bore a quasi-religious cast. They employed myth and symbol, rite and ceremony, scripture and tradition, to make their claims. Every form of magic, superstition, or omen-reading known in the past seems to survive in sophisticated circles. Whole societies may be officially secular, but subcultures and individuals within them are as occupied as ever with ultimate meanings and the signals of the sacred.

Christianity for most of its life has held negative views of other religions. In some epochs it engaged in crusades to extinguish them. In others Christians sent missionaries to woo adherents from these rivals. With one side of their minds, the constituents of the public church today remain wary and critical of the religions in which Christ is not explicitly affirmed. But in another part of their minds and lives, it has become clear that billions of non-Christians are not going to disappear or be converted, and that the world's many centers are going to continue attracting loyalties. Within them, responses to the sacred and the service of humanity have been undertaken too seriously to go unrecognized.

During the Second Vatican Council through its document *Nostra Aetate,* official Catholicism demonstrated its new specific openness to the measures of truth and light that it sees in non-Christian faiths. The church then set out to balance the drive to convert the uncommitted with efforts to become partners in humane causes with holders of other faiths. Mainline Protestantism has also worked strenuously to team with such religions toward common goals, though often at the expense of further efforts to see the circle of believers in Christ extended. Evangelicals have retained the energy and expertise to carry on missionary activity, though many have done so in a spirit of condescension and even hostility to the religious who are not Christian. This spirit carried some of them so far that they even neglected biblical motifs which asserted that God was active among the nations and in the human conscience.

The elements in the public church, therefore, have begun to find a need for one another, for the sake of their calling in a world of increasing interreligious tensions. In America, where ties to Jews as heirs of the divine covenant are both most promising and most complex, the public church stands the best chance of combining its missions of speaking and listening to them. It mediates between those on one hand who see no difference between covenants dependent upon or apart from Christ and on the other hand those who would pounce and prey on Jews because they see no integrity in Judaism except as a breeding ground for Christian proselytes.

A third governing assumption that evokes a need for an awakened public church has to do with how religions today are organizing around three models. One of these we can call *totalist,* as it displays itself in Chinese Maoism, Shi'ite Islam, some African nations, or wherever leaders make efforts to impose a complete set of norms on lives. Theocracies are not a thing of the past. Most philosophers of history of this century, when they look out at the chaos that seems so threatening to whole populations, have envisioned the rise of new prophets and movements which would fabricate religious frameworks in order to coerce peoples. Unless checked by unforeseen forces, they may dominate in the twenty-first century. Sociologist Emile Durkheim saw religion as the collective representation of the life of a people. The prophets of secularity had thought that peoples could get along without such symbols. Now it is evident that if one wishes to impose social control, there is no way to legitimate it without at least a quasi-religious outlook. The public church may be a very frail instrument for countering totalism abroad or in a traumatized America of tomorrow, but it is still called to a responsible witness against repressive politics and impulses.

Another way in which religion today is organizing itself is on *tribalist* lines. Modernity erodes the spiritual boundaries around peoples, yet humans seem to need sharp definitions in order to know who they are, in the fashionable phrase, to "find their identity." Only then can they know whom to trust and to whom they should extend their loyalties. Not until they have such defined psychic boundaries can they find the means to defend their own power and place against real or imagined threats of other people. The prophets of secularity pictured that the form of the tribe would give way to the city and that the people of tomorrow would freely interact. On a world scale the opposite is happening. There are gigantic, passionate efforts to form fierce self-protective tribes. The Basques in Spain, the Gush Emunim in Israel, the Shi'ites in Iran, the Protestants and Catholics in Northern Ireland, the Hindus in Kerala and West Bengal, the *soka gakkai* in Japan, even the Jural people in Switzerland, and the militant fundamentalists in the United States are examples of the trend. In a world of new weapons for terrorism the new tribalism jeopardizes peace and security. The public church seems defenseless in the face of it, since most people have not yet learned to put as much passion and staying power in open-ended religio-ethnic-cultural combinations as in attempts to form tribes whose members will see all outsiders as devils. But the odds against such a public church only increase the urgency of need for it. The public church should focus the "passion for openness" among its adherents, though every trend around is against it.

In free societies a third mode of organizing the religious reality militates against the public church as church. This is the *privatist* solution, the complete individualism of religious choice and practice that modernity urges. Religion in this case has and knows and needs no communal support at all. It is merely a private affair, a subject of pure choice and consumer control, lacking all social consequence or power. Such private religion is an expression of freedom that brings some felt benefits to the people who hold it. From the Christian point of view, however, such religiosity represents problems since the faith is intrinsically communal and it seeks expression as the one body of which Christ is the head. The atomism of private faith, in which "the communion of communions" disappears, also makes individuals fair game for totalist and tribalist movements. Later we shall see how a "hunger for wholeness" marked Weimar Germany. Millions of citizens soon after gorged themselves with the symbols of a demonic totalism that wore a religious guise. The American public church is more vulnerable to privatism than are enclosed and sectarian religious movements to its right. The public church allows for greater freedom of choice than do belligerent Christian absolutisms. But as church it is also to be a witness to the communal character of faith and it possesses resources for promoting the social dimensions of Christian response.

To think that the public church, especially inside American pluralism, can serve as an alternative or counterforce to these three modes around the world may seem fanciful at best and outrageous at worst. Totalist regimes, backed by religion, in our time link with weapons. Their agents kill millions and suppress millions more. The totalitarian who wields the sacred symbols evokes passions that few are able to withstand. Tribalist religion, meanwhile, evokes blood and soil and appeals to primal urges. The passion in tribalism is of a furious sort that the open churches cannot muster. No outsider can penetrate tribal units or weaken their members' hold on reality. Even privatism can often summon fanaticisms because it is a form of concentrating all the energies of an individual on a desperately chosen system of meaning. The public church, meanwhile, is confusing to some because it calls individuals to be alert to the validity of meanings that do not arise in their own circles.

The end of the Age of Enlightenment may well be at hand. Almost nowhere in the world are there trends toward toleration. The tribes are as murderous as ever. Nowhere that I can think of do faiths that allow for complexity and ambiguity compete evenly with those that engage in simplisms or are authoritarian. So apparent is this, and so ominous should it be to anyone who hoped for a world of interactive peoples with common eagernesses to survive, that the public church will need all the passion it can summon if it is to make its alternatives visible.

A law of history is emerging: totalism and tribalism in religion now prosper, while the open forms of response fall victim. Christians do not live by laws of history, however, but by responsible action. Presently they find themselves summoned to help propose an epochal shift in human sensibilities. In this shift, people would learn to combine religious commitment with civility, spiritual passion with a public sense. To help produce a culture in which such combinations might emerge would by itself be a full-time calling for those constituents of the public church who have lost morale or a sense of mission.

The public church does not want to stand alone in the world. In this particular cause one would expect it to find company among those of humanist outlook who fear persecution and dominance by religionists. To date the humanist performance has been disappointing. Many in whom the religious chord does not vibrate have a hard time realizing that for most of the world's billions it does. They constantly underestimate the survival power of religion. Others have a naive prescription: leave religion alone and it will go away and all will be well. But religion will not go away nor would all necessarily be well if it did. Where the historic creeds have disappeared, new faiths have emerged. Moderns no less than their ancestors have shown a desperate need to make sense of their lives. If inherited symbols do not work they erect new ones. The cross and the crescent may suffer but then the hammer and sickle, swastika, or dollar sign summon the absolute loyalties of millions. There seems to be no neutral territory where whole populations can permanently organize themselves without something like religion.

The humanist bystanders have been least helpful when they assume that by definition religion must persecute. They express a kind of macho awe for people who have found faiths powerful enough to lead them to kill. They accompany this expression with taunts against any who believe that in the human future there will be and there must be emergent faiths in a God who is not a god of prey and pounce. They do not allow for loyalty to a God who does not license the people to find value only in their totality, their tribe, their private zealotry. To inform this humanist community of the probable terrors of the future and the need to find new forms of faith communities is a task that will occupy energies of the public church tomorrow.

In the governing assumptions here I have included the validity of Christian faith and community. Libraries full of books defend or call into question their validity. This does not happen to be one of those books. Here there will be no proofs for the existence of God, no philosophical banishments of the problem of evil, no apologies for Jesus Christ as way, truth, and life. Instead the faith and the church appear provisionally as givens. Some urgent questions are bracketed, and the questions move to: *if* people believe, how do they express faith; *if* people are to believe together, how do they organize their common life?

While such bracketing can come with good grace since not all arguments have to take up the same topic, a hidden *hybris*, a smuggled pride is present with the assumption. The notion that this convergence of American Christians could make a difference in establishing the forms of witness for tomorrow seems to overinflate its importance. America does not count for much in the totalist and tribalist worlds, and the freedom its citizens have and use to develop only private faith will further diminish its potency. Also in America, Christianity as a whole has limits that church members often fail to see, and it also does not count for much. Within American Christianity the public church is hard to define, to mobilize, to put into action. Funds are available for asserting the power of tiny well-defined cults. Millions of dollars are available for militant Christians. The oil billionaires may well raise a billion dollars to convert the world to Jesus in their rather tribal scheme. The only kind of power they understand, a fund drive, would not gather much for the delicate and diffuse programs of the public church.

Because of its realism, such an assessment of powerlessness can stun and depress. But in the words of the often bleak American poet Dave Smith, one can say, "Passion, if you once believe in it, is a way of hope." Passions for Christ, for church, for public, for ways to bring them together can animate hopes against hope. They will never produce optimism. The emergence of religious liberty and affirmations of religious pluralism make up a very late, very rare, possibly highly temporary, and certainly gossamer-thin membrane of civility. Many of the once-civil no longer believe in it themselves. The experiment is over. History gives no assurance of the survival of civility, and the promises of God by which Christians live do not picture their causes prevailing or the opposition to them disappearing inside history. Christians are only called to faithfulness, not to read the odds.

Another apologia is in place alongside this confronting of *hybris*. By what right does an historian who is a participant observer of the public church, step outside the reportorial role? Such an historian is able to survive and will never run out of subject matter as a chronicler if the public church withers or is suppressed. The totalist and tribalist versions of religion are more bloodthirsty and thus more interesting subject matter. The privatist versions are more entrepreneurial and thus more sparkling in the history books. But, more important than questions that go with his vocation, by what right does he suggest that participants in the public church should increase their discernment of it and focus energies for an experiment with it?

Some mainline Protestants are certain to read this analysis and urging as an attempt to web them into alliances they do not welcome. The mainline left finds ties to some sorts of Catholics and evangelicals threatening. These Christians might lead people in the more exposed mainline to devote more energy to being church than to being public, to special interiority than to specific openness. Orthodoxy, authoritarianism, antiquarianism, and other blights could come with such a move. Pretend rival evangelicalism and Catholicism away, and they will go away. Some day the rational world will see the virtues of a mainline faith, and on that day, the efforts to build liaisons with other components of the church will appear to have been merely pragmatic and strategic.

To such critics it must be said that mainline Protestantism was itself born evangelical and it has always professed a Catholic dimension. Through the turn-of-the-century decades in which modernisms and liberalisms dominated the mainline elites, most of the laity were still being converted and nurtured through appeals that deserve the name evangelical. Today, as always, most people in mainline churches retain their Christian loyalty through the beating of an evangelical "Gospel-centered" heart. And while pre-Vatican II Roman Catholicism offended most of them, they were at the same time the element in Protestantism that kept to a most Catholic view of culture. Their hymn books and liturgies also reflected their own Catholic past and kinships. They met openly with Catholic Christians in the larger culture. To find them now becoming explicit about evangelical catholicity is to see them recover their roots. To deny these roots would be to overlook these participants' cherished ways of incorporating the openness of the adaptive mainline style along with the prophetic dimensions of Protestant life.

The second set of critics could come from the evangelical flank. Why interrupt us while we are prospering? These are *our* decades. We have overtaken the mainline and are doing most of the growing. Any effort to link us with other Christians must be born of your sense of panic or defeat: if you cannot beat the evangelicals, join them or join with them. Use evangelical successes to distract from defeats among old-stock Protestants. A mainliner's appeal for liaison has to be born of a lust for power or of a desire to assure a larger cohort of Christians while the mainline dwindles. In any case, following the domino theories, to allow any influence on the part of the mainline would foul the evangelical nest; for us to fall enough to adopt any part of an alien program would be to topple entirely. As for links to Catholicism, it is the historic enemy. Evangelicalism has always used Catholicism to define itself negatively. Even though the public church is not considered to be even a formal alliance or entente, its informal linking would compromise us.

To such evangelicals it must be said that evangelicalism has, willy-nilly, moved into the mainstream. Its prosperity has made it a sort of new mainline. Its public relations trumpeters already claim that they have taken over American religion. When the President of the United States, the wealthy people of the Sunbelt, and the celebrities, all announce themselves as Born Again, one can no longer describe evangelicalism as culturally marginal or protected. Evangelical social critics have occupied the space that mainline critics once held by themselves. What is more, one side of evangelicalism has always had the mien and openness of the public church. During the nineteenth century its ancestors even set out to shape the whole public culture, without showing much spirit of defensiveness. Evangelicalism and fundamentalism are by no means the same thing. Some of today's evangelicals are heirs of the nineteenth-century mainstream. Others are repentant descendants of cruder fundamentalist diversions from it. As for Catholicism, I am not prescribing a relation that is wholly new. For years Catholics and evangelicals have been engaging in conversations and interactions which both often describe as more promising than the more familiar encounters they have had with mainline Protestants. The recent moderate evangelicals' reentry into the Protestant mainstream and the beginning of conversation with Catholics will involve them in a movement to a terrain where mainline Protestants are already at home.

Catholicism today is factionalized, so there could be several competing kinds of criticism for the public church idea. Liberal Catholics, who these years are digging in to outlast Pope John Paul II when he asserts the "special interiority" but who feel close to him when he demonstrates the "specific openness" of Catholicism, will feel that ties to the more authoritarian evangelicals would find them playing into the wrong hands. Traditionalist Catholics, on the other hand, who welcome authoritarianism and hope for more of it from the Pope, abhor mainline Protestantism for its liberal admixtures, and want nothing to do with it. But the broad stream of Catholics have learned from experience in other ages and other countries how to be custodians of culture. For a couple of decades they have been as much in the American mainstream as have mainline Protestants. And when Catholics hear evangelicals identify themselves, they find much of the definition to be congenial.

I have not thus far defined these three components. By Catholic I mean the broad stream of faithful American Roman Catholics who are not part of the polarized minorities. Catholic, of course, also implies a dimension of all mainline Protestantism, especially as found in its Anglican and Lutheran versions, though that will not be the accent here. And it characterizes Eastern Orthodoxy, which has a public aspect as well. By evangelical we mean those Protestants who stress the personal experience of conversion, the high authority of the Bible, and the mandate to evangelize others. Mainline Protestant here means that collection of churches whose confessions affirm the historic Christian core faith as it was re-formed in the sixteenth century, and who have chosen to give more attention to nurture than to conversion. Their theology incorporates a vision of public order alongside that of personal conversion.

Each of these three components is itself a communion of communions. Some of these subcommunions create problems for others whose participants wish to be part of the public church. Yet they do not feel free to break their ties to each other, since the public church is a zone, not a formal division within the ranks or something formed by a schism. Thus the Catholics in the public church may sometimes chafe, but they do not divorce themselves from the magisterium or teaching office of the church, an office that includes teachings that are offensive to Protestants and that they do not themselves comfortably live with—especially papal infallibility. This internal tension in Catholicism prevents Catholics from moving with total ease in the public church, a factor that should be creative.

American evangelicals have within their churches and larger communion huge elements that cherish a counterpart to papal infallibility, a concept now called biblical inerrancy. By this they mean not only the authority of the Bible in all matters of faith, but also the complete accuracy of its original manuscripts in matters of geography, science, and history. No one can find out whether one-third, one-half, or two-thirds of the people called evangelical find this view of inerrancy to be correct or integral for defining their church life. The posing of questions about it by poll-takers allows for too many interpretations to be clarifying. A more important question is not how many can live with it, but rather how many insist on using it as a weapon or how many find it congenial as an instrument for studying scripture? Millions who uphold it as a doctrine have given evidence that they find life in the public church congenial. They understand that it offends others there the way infallibility offends the non-Catholics who do not remove themselves because of it. (An inoffensive church is a contradiction in terms.) But those who use it as a weapon in church politics, to divide and purge and conquer, will never want to exemplify "specific openness" to other Christians or to a public in the public church in any case.

Many mainline Protestants, whose chief body of affirmations derives from the same biblical and traditional roots as do those of evangelicals and Catholics, support outlooks that will offend many

participants from the other components. Without question, these
have been Protestants especially responsive to testimony from the
secular culture. They have been so not as a matter of cheap compromise but out of profound theological commitment. They have
read that the *logos* or Word of God who came into the world in the
flesh of Jesus Christ is also "the true light that enlightens everyone."
They have heard that "all things were created through him and for
him and he is before all things," and that they have to be alert for
surprising meanings in these "all things." To some evangelicals
and Catholics this alertness by itself is not an issue. What specific
mainliners do with it is; and their partners will often be offended,
not by the theological proposition that they should be alert to the
Christian import in the larger creation, but by the character of the
response.

Tensions exist and will remain in the mainline, Catholic, and
evangelical components, and they will carry these into some conflicts within the public church. But all this contesting can be creative, since thoughtful people in each component have already recognized the gifts the others bring. Were they to divorce themselves
from their own colleagues who stress "special interiority" over
"specific openness," they might lose their own genius. All three
traditions have seen such dissolutions in their past. The
evangelicalism of revivalist awakening is often a one-generation
phenomenon. Mainline Protestantism and Catholicism have often
simply bled off into the larger culture. Where the offensively assertive evangelicals, Catholics, and mainline Protestants do not alienate
or purge their more open colleagues, they can provide strengths.
Meanwhile, the public church constituents can rescue their fellow
believers "back home" from defeating provincialisms.

This ecumenical model sees Catholics, evangelicals, and mainline
Protestants in symbiotic relations. My model is a churchly counterpart to a political one provided centuries ago by Johannes Althusius,
a Dutch Calvinist humanist. He detailed the concept of a political
counterpart, a "community of communities" in the polis, the human
city, that is also appropriate in the ecclesia, the church. Keeping the
original Greek, he spoke of the components as *symbiotes,* who
"pledge themselves each to the other, *by explicit or tacit agreement*
[emphasis mine], to mutual communication of whatever is useful and
necessary for the harmonious exercise of social life," or now, in this
case, Christian life. When the word "components" appears, I invite
the reader to think of them as *symbiotes,* human elements that live
together and off one another's contributions in the family of apostolic
churches. Most of the time, in Althusius's term, their agreements will

be tacit, but no less vital for that. The world and the church may not now need a new ecumenical committee document to be proposed for explicit agreement.

Timing is always a problem in issues of discernment and definition. To some humanists, talk of the public church would be premature or phony, because they are not convinced that the ecumenical movement ever was more than a public relations gesture or an attempt by declining churches to cut their losses by federating or uniting. These humanists have shown that they lack the ability to see how people can combine commitment to Christ with life in traditions where believers grasp their commitments in different ways. These differences should lead to killing, in any worthwhile religion, say the historically informed outsiders. Or others would say, common commitments should mean the end of all denominational or tribal lines, shouldn't they? But to those outside the church who have observed how the participants in the movement have attempted to be faithful to the biblical mandates and promises about the original and final oneness of the church, the public church will properly appear to be a refinement, not a departure.

Some mainline Protestants froze their view of conservative Protestants in the pattern of the 1740s, when liberal Charles Chauncy scorned the "new light" ways of Jonathan Edwards as being dangerously emotional. Others chose the model of 1925, when William Jennings Bryan at the Scopes Trial embodied fossilized faith. To these, evangelicalism is nothing but a cosmetic version of fundamentalism, a public relations gesture itself. Evangelical prosperity these days is then only a symptom of the cancer to which a sensation-hungry and antirational world has fallen victim. They have not noticed the Catholic varieties of evangelicalism, so they try to force all evangelicals into a single mold. Even strategically this displays no more wisdom then Americans showed in the 1950s when they extended all socialisms from the die of "atheistic Communism." Theologically it also does not do justice to the Christian amplitude of evangelicalism.

To those Catholics who believe that "the final logic of Protestantism is atheism" and who are *integristes* about papal authority, both evangelicals and mainline Protestants are repulsive. They seem unneeded because Catholicism is half a billion strong, and they are unwanted as distractions. But such Catholics have not read their own orthodox and official Vatican II documents on the Christian validities within the communions separate from Rome. They have not participated in theological conversations in congregations or seminaries, where surprising commonalities have appeared.

Timing by decades: in the 1950s in America mainline Protestants got together, in the 1960s they and Catholics found each other, and in the 1970s pioneers in all three camps recognized mutualities. What is needed now is not one more reportorial treatise on the prosperities or declines within the three, but one on the prospects for their life together. This is not a book of personal testimony, but I could easily convert it into one by pointing to the evidences of the public church. Most of the fruitful engagements in recent years on Christian soil, whether among youth and students or among laity or between congregations, have been at the juncture where "the right of the left and the left of the right" meet. Somehow this never turns out to be the bland middle. Restless evangelicals and Catholics on the move display one set of energies, while mainline Protestants and liberal Catholics now busy retracing their own roots and defining their own loyalties, find company with each other. To some critics it may look as if the evangelicals are there to be schooled by the mainline Protestants in techniques at getting public notice. To others it may seem as if mainline Protestants are hitchhiking on evangelical wagons in order to ride back to a past from our day, when "roots" are popular. But the revisions in all three camps have drawn upon the same impulses of Christians to read both the traditions and the times. Now it is a fruitful moment for them to become more conscious of each other as *symbiotes* in the political community of communities and in the family of apostolic churches.

As for the term "public church," it fits in a larger context of uses of the word public, so some pointers if not full definitions are in order here. Such a church is a partial Christian embodiment within *public religion*. This term from Benjamin Franklin fits the American pluralist pattern better than does Rousseau's "civil religion," because it took into account the particularities of the faiths that would not disappear or lightly merge to please other founders of the nation. These churches could, however, contribute out of their separate resources to public virtue and the common weal. *Public theology* is in my view an effort to interpret the life of a people in the light of a transcendent reference. The people in this case are not simply the church but the pluralism of peoples with whom the language of the church is engaged in a larger way. The *public church*, then, is a specifically Christian polity and witness.

If there are some novelties in the present definition and call, an historian can serve the public church by sketching precedents for this Christian contribution to American public theology as a critical and constructive voice within public religion. This contribution has little to do with "saving faith," which refers to the ways in which a person is finally grounded in or reconciled to God. It focuses on "ordering faith," which helps constitute civil, social, and political life from a theological point of view.

Never from the first European arrivals, has America lacke'd the witness of the public church. The original circumstances differ vastly now from the time when, for a century, there was a Catholic monopoly in the New World or when, for two more, there was a Protestant one in the English colonies. One voice out of many shows the imperial intention. Caspar de la Cruz, a Portuguese Dominican spelled the original vision of ordering within the Christian commonwealth in 1569: "In order that the peoples might be summoned to hear the Gospel, as they ought to be before the end of the world . . . God ordained the discoveries made by the Spaniards in the New World. . . . By these means, God through his servants has converted many peoples . . . until the coming . . . of the overflowing of the peoples . . . under one Pastor as Christ says."

Such a canopy allows for no hint of pluralism in public theology and merely extends to the new world the Constantinian ethos and framework from the old. So it was also with the permanent settlers, the English Protestants. Their public theology was decisively and nationalistic English: "God is so much English," scribbled one promoter of exploration in the New World. And the theocracy was in no way to be pluralist. For John Cotton, pioneer minister, the spiritual and temporal orders were to be "co-ordinate States." When the Puritans talked the language of millennium, it was toward a transformed moral and political order in a Protestant model that expected Christ's return. When these English used the language of a covenant that for the believer was as old as Adam or at least John Calvin, they included little talk of a protected church that had no bearing on public order. In fact, the late Perry Miller even perceived them changing the concept of deity to match their new needs: "For all ordinary purposes [God] has transformed Himself in the covenant into a God vastly different from the inscrutable Divinity of pure Calvinism. He has become a God chained—by His own consent, it is true, but nevertheless a God restricted and circumscribed—a God who can be counted upon, a God who can be lived with. Man can always know where God is and what He intends." This was, said Miller, an "extremely strategic device for arousing human activity."

The ancient Christianizing emperor Constantine and the Puritan blenders of civil and religious life did not have the field to themselves in public theology. From the first decade there were also separationist voices, and their sectarian witness also has a place in precedents for the public church in a pluralist order. Thus Roger

Williams, invited out of Massachusetts Bay in the first decade, was a misfit millenarian who believed that from the time of Christ until the end time the church was unavailable as a pure form. No state could speak for the things of God. His word was radical: "First that the People (the ORIGINAL of all free Power and Government) are not invested with Power from Christ Jesus, to rule His . . . Church, to keep it pure, to punish Opposites by force of Arms, etc. Secondly, that the Pattern of the National Church of Israel, was a None-such, unimitable by any Civil State, in all or any of the Nations of the World beside"—including England and New England. This most radical separatist after 1639 found in New England no church, no covenant, no believers' baptism, only the pure future of the millennium, and witnesses to it among seekers like himself as signs of its coming. The church was "in the wildernesse."

Even this antipublic theology was a form of public theology. Williams continued to counsel Massachusetts Bay and to work for civil concord with the Indians. He defended Indian rights against preempting Christian princes who, he thought, misread public theology and thought they had a claim on Indian land. "The truth is, the great Gods of this world are God-belly, God-peace, God-wealth, God-honour, God-pleasure," and in New England, "God-land." In Williams's critical theology, the basis of government is the people, who have no divine power to govern. God is for government in general as God is for marriage, but God does not endorse particular governments. Government as government has no business with religion at all. Over against those who today think they must elect only their own Born Again fellow believers to rule, their hero Williams wrote: "A Christian Captaine, Christian Merchant, Physitian, Lawyer, Pilot, Father, Master, and (so consequently) Magistrate, etc. is no more a Captaine, Merchant, Physitian, Lawyer, Pilot, Father, Master, Magistrate, etc. then a Captaine, Merchant, etc. of any other Conscience or Religion." Nor dare there be Christian Crusades. Christ did approve the "lawfulnesse of conversation with such persons in civill things, with whom it is not lawful to have converse in spirituals," and the Saints and Churches of God might well deal with "Idolatrous and Antichristian" magistrates and people, even whole states and kingdoms. Believers might "lawfully cohabit, and hold civill converse and conversation" with them. And on those terms Williams chartered civility: "I commend that man, whether Jew, or Turk, or Papist, or whoever, that steers no otherwise than his conscience dares."

Williams deserves attention because he is the underside of the Catholic-Protestant covenant that dominated from 1492 to 1789 and maybe longer, through three-fifths of North American history. His critical and antitheocratic theology was still a theology. And it located on dissenters' grounds what the public church recognizes also on other assumptions: "There is a morall vertue, a morall fidelitie, abilities and honestie, which other men (beside Church-members) are, by good nature and education, by good Lawes and good examples nourished and trained up in, that Civill places of Trust and Credit need not to be Monopolized into the hands of Church-Members (who sometimes are not fitted for them) and all others deprived and despoiled of their naturall and Civill Rights and Liberties."

With those as basic oppositions, we can single out precedents for components in the public church of today. The theocratic covenant in which God ruled, prevailed for at least a century longer, and still lived on in the 1740s when the foremost public theologian of the colonial era, revivalist Jonathan Edwards, emerged with his focus on the transcendent backdrop to civil affairs. This progenitor of evangelicalism (and the mainline!), who did so much to modernize religion by promoting personal decision and choice within the covenant, did not write much on political concerns. He did not foresee in Christian terms the nation that was forthcoming. He was a God-intoxicated, religiously possessed thinker who by force of intellect and rhetoric, however, could not but have a bearing on civil order as a member of the revivalist generations.

Edwards, despite his affective reputation, spoke up also for reason, including fallen reason as a restraining grace of God that helps make civil life possible. He affirmed nature, which teaches obedience to God and allows for public life. The preacher spoke for virtue, but it was to be grounded in "benevolence to being in general" and thus was more theological and aesthetic than political. Yet Edwards wanted "great men" of "civil authority" (and "rich men," but we can let that pass by) to promote the work of redemption. "Without order there can be no general direction of a multitude to any particular designed end, their purposes will cross and hinder one another. A multitude cannot act in union one with another without order; confusion separates and divides them, so that there can be no concert or agreement." This was again the theocratic motif. Its content is of little help in pluralistic America, but as a precedent this model demonstrates the concern for public order among evangelical pioneers. "Civil, ecclesiastical and family affairs, and all our personal concerns, are designed and ordered in subordination to a future world, by the Maker and Disposer of all things."

Edwards, like Williams, held a millennial vision but of a much different order. He foresaw "a city compact together," with no nationalism or chauvinism in its makeup. This city would come about without cataclysm, only gradually. For all that Edwards celebrated a faith that America was to be the scene of a new dispensation of providence, he nevertheless remains the judge of those who are merely engrossed in mundane life and forget what he called "this affair of traveling to heaven." But even those travels did not divert him from appropriate concerns for the earthly city.

A century later mainline Protestantism was beginning to establish itself apart from the revivalist tradition. A seminal figure now was Congregationalist minister Horace Bushnell of Hartford. He looked less to conversion and more to nurture for building the commonwealth. As was the case in subsequent liberalism, for him nature and supernature were not opposed but were complementary, making up "the one system of God." Therefore, Bushnell held a positive view of the "foundation of civic obligation" and went in quest of the "holy republic." "I cannot leave politics alone, till I am shown that politics are not under the government of God." He complained that Americans had taken up theories of government which eliminated moral considerations and made of it a mere social compact. He insisted that there had to be a contract "from above," as it were. "We are born into government as we are into the atmosphere, and when we assume to make a government or constitution, we only draw out one that is providentially in us before." Out of such liberal contributions to the mainline also came an Anglo-Saxon view of superiority that today we would find to be racist, one that blighted mainline Protestantism. Later it became clear that the black churches belonged alike to evangelicalism, and the mainline and the racial aspect diminished.

Bushnellian confidence in the moral order did not allow for pluralism as the mainline would insist it should a century later. But just as Edwards with his "traveling to heaven" introduced the transcendent note that has been the evangelical gift of evangelicalism, so Bushnell produced the counterpart, a view of immanence. He showed that ordering and saving faith had something to do with each other: "Legislation wants redemption for its coadjutor, and only through the divine sacrifice, thus ministered, can it ever hope to consummate the proposed obedience. . . . Redemption also wants legislation, to back its tender appeals of sacrifice, by the stern rigors of law. Both together will compose the state of complete government" as cofactors. Half a century later the Social Gospel revised and employed such language. No mainline Protestant heirs would find the old imperialism congenial today, but the rest of this nineteenth-century emphasis did promote concern for redeeming and legislating alike.

The third component, Catholicism, by definition has always been for public theology, though after Protestants came to dominance in America very few Catholic voices were able to gain a hearing here. The hearing came after millions of Roman Catholic people arrived. The word and example of the greatest Catholic prelate, James Cardinal Gibbons of Baltimore, who dominated before and after the turn of the twentieth century was decisive. His Catholic burden was to show that its public theology belonged in a pluralist republic that had been invented chiefly by Protestants and people of the Enlightenment, and this not long after Pope Pius IX had blasted republicanism and religious liberty. Gibbons may have had an administrative style that favored "masterly inactivity," but his theology advocated masterful activity to wed Catholicism as church with a theology for the republic.

Any Catholic who now is uncertain about the legitimacy of a public theology that might issue from the church in America will find courage from Gibbons's precedent, even for his mere at-homeness in the culture. As a constitutionalist the prelate urged that the church must adapt to United States democracy, not to provide a universal model but because it was most congenial here. The Baltimorean did not want to renew church-state ties, and even defended the American model of separation in unfriendly Rome. A nationalist, he ministered to immigrants but was worried about too much heterogeneity: the nation was for him also a community of communities that was in danger of losing its commonality. This view he based in a casual but firm expression of natural law which argued that religion was "the essential basis of civil society." One will find nothing of Williams's critical stance in Gibbons, but at his moment Catholics chiefly needed the assurance that they belonged in American civil and public life, and ever since Gibbons they have not doubted it.

So far we have mentioned the black churches only in passing, but a demonstration that this large component has been at home with the public church concept was clear from the way Martin Luther King easily reached into their heritage. His was a theocentric vision, as he felt "the reality of a personal God" becoming ever deeper. King's witness came at the crest of secular theology in white mainline Protestantism, but his thought centered on the Kingdom of God. "Living in the colony of time, we are ultimately responsible to the idea of eternity. As Christians we must never surrender our supreme loyalty . . . for at the heart of our universe is a higher reality—God and his kingdom of love. . . . The church is challenged to make the gospel of Jesus Christ relevant within the social situation." At the same time, King drew upon the Enlightenment and especially on Jefferson's Declaration of Independence along with the constitutional and Lincolnian traditions as sources of public theology.

The black leader typically related saving and ordering faith: "On the one side the church seeks to change the souls of men and thereby unite them with God; on the other, it seeks to change the environmental conditions of men so that the soul will have a chance after it is changed." Something, he argued, had happened to engulf human nature in a tragic threefold estrangement that separates persons from themselves, their neighbors, and their God. The human journey has brought a moral and spiritual famine in Western civilization. But it is not too late to return home. For King "home" meant "kindredship" in a kingdom that dialectically related love and justice. To promote it, he urged, one may on occasion have to reach for higher law when human law is unjust. King showed his Catholic side by quoting Thomas Aquinas in support of that view, his evangelical aspect by speaking of redemptive conversion, and his mainline element by his own and many exemplifications of "specific openness."

To cite these few but giant exemplars at beginnings or climaxes of traditions is to do little more than plant billboards along the way of the inquiry. No element of the public church could be called back to all of them, since their positions all contradict each other in part, and Williams, for one, counters all the others. But if the early Catholics and Protestants signal the need for Catholic custodianship of the public realm and the dissenters display the Protestant critique, then in Edwards, Bushnell, Gibbons, and King, we find four giants on whom their traditions can call. They do not give detailed prescriptions that anyone can follow today. But they do not permit people in their lineages to retreat from concern for both saving faith and ordering faith. Together these two make up the zones of activity of the public church, which today is taking a new shape. In Althusius's terms, its agreements may remain tacit, but its form and understanding and work must become explicit.

2

A Pilgrimage of Participants

Where is the reality of the public in the spiritual search of Americans today? The prospective participant in the public church sets out on the journey without many landmarks. Most searchers have little knowledge of past pilgrimages. They live in the present without having available a repertoire or repository of options. If one of them has access to the past, it may well be that in our culture this will take the form of the stimulating of nostalgia. But nostalgia is only the rust of memory, the oxidized edge of what once was solid. It can only rouse in people a superficial yearning for "the good old days."

In religious life, the idea of the good old days usually means a time when life was simpler. A fundamental feature of this past was that it offered little or no choice, and thus produced little bewilderment. One kind of young person grew up in a ghetto or a shtetl and never met, or at least was never attracted to, the way of life of a single non-Jew. Everyone in another's part of town was Italian-Catholic, or all other nearby villagers were Irish Catholics, so the young Catholic would not have to cope with anyone of a different ethnic background. In my grandparents' Swiss valley, every person they ever would have met was Swiss, Reformed, and recorded on the register of the one local parish church. In any of these worlds, a single set of symbols was ready to guide people. At least, so says nostalgia. The possessor of such a view of the past seldom thinks of how bored he or she would be to be reencased in the world of the great-grandparent. Such a world seems attractive because one aspect of life in it was resolved. A map was on hand for the spiritual journey. With it, one could be free to put energies into other dimensions of the business of living.

As with all rust, this kind does pick up something from the substance off which it lives. Unquestionably there was more coherence in the world of thought and symbols which surrounded or possessed medieval people than is the case with moderns. But a close-up examination leads one to adopt less simplistic views. Recent researches have shown, for example, that all through the Middle Ages in Christian Europe believers also clung to pagan views that survived from before their peoples had first been baptized. They might hear a Christian message intended to purge their world of evil spirits, but they also took pains to surround themselves with charms and relics to ward off such spirits. The church entered into an uneasy alliance with the manipulators of superstition and often blessed the relics. And the individual did live with some uncertainty over the price to be paid for a double set of assurances.

One instinct of nostalgic people is unerring, however. For most people in the past, compared to most people today, there were overall fewer choices. Modern media of communication and, in literate cultures, forms of higher education now bring a dazzling array of options to the attention of people. Recent wars have carried troops to distant places and brought once-provincial military people in range of others' way of life. Some elements of these repel and others attract. "The heathen" may look stupid. Or the adherents of other religions may embody values we have forgotten or we never had. But in either case, to see that other people live effectively by systems we cannot understand calls into question the value of our systems or the integrity with which we hold them. Some people respond to the challenge by affirming that all systems are equally true. As a consequence, they take none seriously. Others borrow from each and lose their hold on who they are. Still others turn cynical: "What is truth? What is valuable?" No doubt, not many thoughtful people in a free society would agree that the growth of choice by itself was a problem. At first it seems like a solution. We all want it. Most Americans indicate support of an economic free market because they welcome choice and want fewer restrictions. So also in the realm of ideas, only a minority wants to be completely constrictive and to rule out by fiat access to attractive alternatives. Americans erect billboards that urge people to "Go to the Church of Your Choice." Foreign visitors a century after Lord James Bryce visited America still find what he found. There seem to be "no two opinions": all citizens affirm the voluntary system of religious options, in which people are free to pick and choose or reject. Americans look at Maoism, the Shi'ite Islam of the Ayatollah Khomeini, or theocracies and say, with total predictability, that they do not want replicas of these. In morality, except in a few selected cases, most free citizens are "prochoice." In the arts, they do not want to have a style imposed on them. They know what they like. People usually do not like to have the art of the public square chosen by experts who know what is best for them. So they protest, desecrate the art, or grudgingly accommodate themselves to it—and take refuge from it by expressing their own taste on their living room walls.

The drift of religion today is, if anything, moving toward an utterly free market in which little trace of fate, election, or predestination remains. Television evangelists act as if none of their hearers had pasts, as if their viewers were acting with a clean slate so far as spiritual alternatives are concerned. Twenty-five minutes later, the enlightened among them are supposed to have "chosen" a decision for Christ (genus) through a particular set of devices of that particular evangelist (species). And along with that decision, the convert repudiates others. Where once a congregation transmitted its life through the several generations, now a clientele forms around a passing celebrity of its choice. Religion is an item that one consumes, not a reality which possesses people. The consumer "uses it up" and constantly needs a new quantity.

What is a person to do in the face of such constant and instant appeals? Any surveyor of the culture can find great numbers who simply drop out into drugs or disco culture—or apathy. Franz Kafka once told of a "hunger artist" who made his living in a carnival as a professional faster. People paid to see how long he could go without food. Finally, as he neared death, he confessed why he had gone into this line of work: he never could find the food he liked. Some people pass all the cafeteria lines of religious choice and keep their distance from them.

An alternative for others is to sample all the offerings, taking a dab of Eastern religion and a dibble of Western mysticism; add a dash of African seasoning and a dribble of occult dressing. This is an aesthetic approach which implies intimacy with a spiritual lore but never commitment. The sampler can also take the choices sequentially, moving from a stage of commitment to one into a stage of layering, of adding on another, or rejecting what one was previously "into." More popular than these ways, however, is the decision to cancel out all choice by restricting oneself to a single dish, say, fast-food fare. Such a chooser has found the "one way" and allows for no virtue in any other. Those who pass down the cafeteria line want choice but they pay a price for their freedom. Continuity in spiritual life can lead to boredom, and what is solid fare is too demanding. To deride people in these circumstances is easy, but it is more important to understand them. They are well represented among the offspring of mainline Protestants, among newly arrived evangelicals now exposed to an alluring culture, and to restless Catholics; and also to their elders who at midlife sense a yearning, sometimes a desperation, to be better placed or rooted than they were.

Modernity is a story of choice based on progressive sunderings, "choppings up" of existence. These are familiar in the sociological literature that sets out to account for our times. Adult life, it says, severs one from the childhood scene. The artist lacks rootage and is cut off from the groundwork of the earth. Chance separates people from secure authority. Industry pulls apart one's residence and one's work. The scholars distinguish between value and fact. The practitioners divide practice from theory. The artists devise art for its own sake and split it off from communal values or belief. One is never sure but that a person walking nearby does not inhabit a world that is different in every way from one's own. There are no signs, symbols, or languages to communicate across the boundaries that separate world views create.

So with religion. It ministers to one part of life, but not another. Public life divorces itself from private faith. One should not mingle religion and politics or economics. The litany goes on: I cannot connect the faith I know on weekends with my job during the week. One set of values connects me to family life, but this conflicts with the competitive values that animate my market life. In public endeavor I am called to cooperate with fellow citizens, but in private enterprise I am to do them in, or be eaten alive. God is in a box marked sacred, and most activity is in a box marked secular. But the sacred box is itself divided into compartments, and the psychiatrist, syndicated columnist counselor, and therapist all invade the compartment once reserved for religion.

Problems result for all the traditional roles of the church, which suddenly is on the defensive. Theology, the interpretation of the life and language of a people, breaks down because there is no communion of people, there are only private strivers. To whom is the act of preaching to be directed, if the audience is made up of people each of whom has already established a trajectory of life, and who present themselves in a congregation only so long as the message conveniently reaches an individual on that particular course? The audience turns out to be segmented, and is not really a congregation. The congregational style then changes and becomes a loosely connected set of specialities. One person is part of an Alcoholics Anonymous extension but has nothing to do with another who is in the Migratory Worker cause, while neither connects with the hobbyist who cares about forms of worship. And the animating spirituality is also chopped up, since the congregation must allow for charismatic and anticharismatic factions, followers of a *cursillo* and rejecters thereof, along with insistences on various "one ways."

This description soon turns to stereotype at best and melodrama at worst. No one really wants to repeal the choice or knows how to roll back the process of "chopping up," in order to retrieve the world that appeals to the nostalgic. And the public church, forbidden to engage in false advertising, enters the scene with a message that is designed to dispel illusions. The past was never so neat, so rich in organismic ethos. And the faith of Christians was certainly not born in an integrated and whole world. Nor will that faith now lead one to a life that excludes further demands or confusing choices.

The dose of historical realism insists that early Christians were members of *paroikiae*, parishes, which meant precisely gatherings of sojourners in alien cities like our own. They had the advantage of recognizing the sign of the one cross of Christ over against all the other signals. But they also brought along various backgrounds and world views. The New Testament gives tantalizing glimpses of these. Leaders urged them to "be of one mind" or to "have the mind of Christ among themselves," but these very phrases alert readers to the fact that the urging was necessary. Christians did not come together with and probably never found a simplifying "one mind." Edward Gibbons describes their surrounding world as one in which the people saw all religions to be equally true, the philosophers found them to be equally false, and the magistrate regarded them as equally useful. Christians just barely managed to get their variety of outlooks together enough to have themselves persecuted. When Constantine and later Theodosius (380 C.E.) made Christianity the official cultus of the Empire and then ruled out others, they did not succeed in eliminating choice. Pagan vestiges and revivals survived, and there were barbarian intrusions or transformations and debates over every vital Christian teaching or rite. Where there was uniformity, it resulted from coercion. The sword alone did what unifying rhetoric could never accomplish.

Today it still takes the sword or the brainwash to eliminate variety and choice. Marxist and Maoist regimes replicate those that they replace by acts of "demodernizing," which means seeking to shape a wholistic outlook on life and eliminating choice for subjects. The thoughtful pilgrim rarely is ready to settle for this kind of alternative. So the bearer of the public church's message and way has no choice but to encounter seekers with the realistic word: to become part of its company is not to find the elimination of choice but to learn to live with it and in spite of its possible confusions.

Those who have read widely in sociology will have discerned in these paragraphs the shadows of influence by thinkers like Max Weber or Talcott Parsons and, in our generation, Peter Berger or John Murray Cuddihy. For our course and map, it was necessary to extract notions from them almost to the point of caricature, so they need take no responsibility nor should they be faulted for a thousand subtleties left out. And by our choice of language, familiar words like "differentiation, specialization, universalization, or pluralization of life worlds" turned out in translation to be words like "chopped up." But from the midst of these borrowings one sentence of Cuddihy leaps out and demands exact quotation: "Differentiation slices through ancient primordial ties and identities, leaving crises and 'wholeness-hunger' in its wake."

Wholeness-hunger: that term may well summarize the ageless spiritual quest. Whether or not modernity changes the concept completely, there is now an evident intensifying of such hunger. Cuddihy, in a footnote, helps us track the term to its unlikely source in historian Peter Gay's treatment of pre-Hitler Weimar Germany. Gay and the Weimar Germans took bigger gulps of the cosmos and drank headier aesthetic brews than do most Americans, so our foray into their world may throw the search against a larger screen than many of us find congenial. But before we compromise it away and cut it to the size of our mundane lives, we hear it out.

Gay traces the language of wholeness-hunger to the poetry of Friederich Hölderlin and his *Hyperion,* with a reference to what was then believed by Germans to be a Germanic monopoly: "It is a hard saying, and yet I say it because it is the truth: I can conceive of no people more dismembered than the Germans. You see workmen but no human beings, thinkers but no human beings, priests but no human beings, masters and servants, youths and staid people, but no human beings." Felix Gilbert says of all this that Hölderlin bid "for a new wholeness of life." The romantic German youth movements sang its praise and went tracking it in summer camps and mountain retreats. One of the folk *Lieder* sang of "the whole man, complete unto himself"—*in sich geschlossen*—not distracted by choice or external bids.

Philosopher Paul Natorp entered a futile warning against the irrational and totalist possibilities in this search, since it spoke only of soul and severed the soul from the mind, and thus from criticism. The warning, thinkers in the public church might say, remains in place, for irrational soul-search can still crave totalism. "The Bible says . . . The pope says . . . My therapist says . . ." In bumper-sticker language: "God said it. I believe it. That settles it." In political language: "We need a leader who will decide right from wrong. We need a Christian culture that will let us have only true values and textbooks." So Natorp: "You fear the dismemberment of your being in all the piecework of human wishing and knowing, and fail to notice that you cannot achieve wholeness if you reject such large and essential parts of that which has been allotted to all mankind. You seek the indivisibility of man's being, and yet assent to its being torn apart." For, in the end, the totalist who exploits wholeness-hunger does tear apart the human absorptive capacity from the critical, the devouring soul from the inquiring mind.

In America both the language of wholeness-hunger and criticism of it come in more muted and compromising tones which are less likely to put us off. They refer to a scale and scope in which citizens can locate themselves. The distinctive American (and possibly modern European) feature may seem a surprising emphasis. I see it as being analogous to a feature that Daniel Bell has pointed to in response to the welfare society. He has spoken of "entitlement," a sense people develop that they are entitled to certain rights and benefits that were once beyond the range of human possibility or regarded as the luxury of royalty and the landed rich.

People feel they are "entitled" to long life and health care in all its stages. They are entitled to personal and social security. If an earthquake or flood comes, they are not merely the helpless victims people once were. They are entitled to federal loans to help them get started again. The children of poor and unmarried mothers are entitled to support against the starvation their counterparts elsewhere always knew. Veterans are entitled to benefits that the legless and the blind among their kind once were denied. Everyone is entitled to a good education, a minimum wage. Citizens have come to take these entitlements for granted and they debate only the amounts, the efficiency of their delivery, the equitability of their disposal. Lest anyone be politically distracted from the flow of argument by this paragraph, let me say that I am not among those who call these entitlements into basic question in a prosperous society, but join those who would make the case for these extensions of "rights" in an industrialized world. The subject appears here both as a metaphor and as a conducive agent to carry over entitlement into another realm, the spiritual.

People in free societies today live by spiritual entitlement. While my reading is not as wide or deep as it might be in other religions, what has leaped out at me there is the general absence of promise. The journey of life has a goal, but what measure of attainment one reaches is not assured. Always ahead is nirvana, enlightenment, the *visio dei,* ataraxy, fulfillment. The popular versions of Eastern religion that come packaged in the West admit of too easy, too advertisable, guaranteed benefits. A wider and deeper, indeed lifelong, reading in biblical faith leads to the awareness that Hebrew and Christian scriptures, the charter documents of Christian churches, are not unambiguous about entitlement. Of course, one can excerpt isolated passages and use them as proof-texts to suggest that "fish are jumpin' and abundant livin' is easy." But, read on.

The primordial heroes of faith, whose careers chapter eleven of the Letter to the Hebrews in the New Testament recapitulates, did not live by entitlement and fulfilled wholeness. Provisionally, let us accept the interpretation of their faith-careers by the writer to Hebrews, since these are offered as exemplars to Christian pilgrims. Abel "received approval" of God, and though he died, through his faith he is still speaking. But was not Abel entitled to a long life, exempt from violent death at the hand of his brother? Enoch walked with God and was taken away at the ripe young age of 365, using the numbering of Genesis. But in the modern spirit of entitlement, Enoch would have felt God owed him the years apportioned his son Methuselah, which were 969. Noah was rescued with his household, but lived not only by a covenant—which offers wholeness—but also with a famed curse.

Abraham was entitled to a land called promised but he lived only in tents, with the continuing promise of a city. And Sarah bore a child, but if she was entitled to mere pleasures, these were denied her. Isaac and Jacob, likewise. Moses was entitled to a promised land and "kept the Passover" but only saw and never occupied that land. By the time the writer of Hebrews got bored, ran out of space, or had made his point, he was running through a phone book: "Gideon, Barak, Samson, Jephthah, David, Samuel and the prophets . . ." They may have been heroic, but a rereading of the story of Jephthah does not show entitlement rewarded. Samuel had his disappointments. The Davidic lore is full of brokenness, to the end. And the writer might have mentioned Job.

Or Jesus, "who for the joy that was set before him endured the cross, despising shame." And if the writer to the Hebrews sees Jesus with a happy ending, it came beyond history, not this side of the inescapable cross. "Father, if it be thy will, take this cup from me . . ." is far from the language of one entitled.

Yet a commercial and consumerist culture turns this all around. If one evangelist in thirty minutes does not convert, heal, and give possessions, there is another on a competing channel. If one bestseller on the airport newsstand does not succeed in producing instant nirvana, spin the stand and another will. So says the promise. If one therapy does not resolve all conflicts and overcome all brokenness, another "holistic" approach is certain to. They have advertised that they can. Someone will put the consumer in perfect touch with herself, her self-esteem, nature, oneness, lovers, and God. By birthright, moderns—shall we fault them or only understand them, ourselves?—feel entitled to such wholeness.

The hunger for wholeness, felt by the heroes of faith and modern consumers or seekers alike, has ontological roots. Translated to the language of theology, Augustine's word is still the classic: "Thou hast made us for thyself and our hearts are restless until they find their rest in thee." This hunger is in the pattern of biblical revelation. People seek what relates to the root *yasha'*: rescue from straits, achieved deliverance, room to breathe. They seek *shalom,* which is far from mere absence of war and is a profound positive peace. Eschatology ministers to the hunger, for "in the end" we shall be given to see what is not now apparent, that "in Christ . . . all things hold together," cohere in wholeness (Colossians 1:17). And this hunger is central to the mystical search, for one to be absorbed in the All, the *unum,* the One. The hunger belongs to the species, but most of its members until now had to learn to live with denial or partial fulfillment. Moderns, offered so many advertised benefits and having freedom to choose in the midst of a chopped-up existence, expect more.

Readings of American history, in versions that content themselves with the legendary or that come from the distance of a vision, show how persistent the thirst for wholeness has been. The Native American, certainly in image and more in reality than can be known today, lived and sought to live in harmony with nature and the spirits to which nature was somehow transparent. Rites were designed to overcome a misfit between humans and nature.

Almost five hundred years ago, Euro-America was born as a reality called Catholic. And Catholicism appeals to the search for wholeness through its double meanings: it was universal, designed to grasp all humanity. And it penetrated all dimensions of being (*kata holos,* "through the whole") in all the ways from conquest to mission to celebration.

The English third chapter was devoted to the dream of an organic and covenanted community. The Puritans were realists about the promise and its fulfilment, but they took pains to knit their intentions together, so that no detail escaped their scope or interpretation. The giant of the Great Awakening, Jonathan Edwards, took his futile stand against a chopping up of the interior life. He converted people to the new covenant, pleading and arguing that "reason" and the "affections" were not at war with each other, since both were grounded in the Great Being and thus could not be in contradiction. Later revivalists permitted, indeed they encouraged, the chopping up by stressing emotion and experience at the expense of reason, which was the accursed part of the human. And their contemporary Enlightenment leaders, more than they wished, chopped up the human by elevating reason and qualifying, though not denying, the affections and passions. The two confronted their heirs with cruel choice and almost inevitable *Halbheit,* halfness, division. The emotive revivalists a century later had to promise wholeness in the millennial kingdom, while the dispassionate enlightened folk envisioned, with Jefferson, a romantic agrarian setting to promote simplicity and nature. He and Benjamin Franklin, therefore, touted a "public religion," which for Franklin meant a meshing or integrating of what was good in the sects and for Jefferson meant the displacement of old sects by this new, republican one.

In the midst of urban brokenness, Social Gospel leaders later offered a social and ecumenical Kingdom of God, which would overcome the clashes between classes and sects. Many people did not read their spiritual search into this promise but the social vision was pure and graspable.

Of course, there has been a critical alternative, apparent in the dark side of Edwards and Jefferson alike, men who did not feel they could finally overcome within history the afflicting brokenness. Abraham Lincoln appealed to transcendent reality for the nation while recognizing that wounds were never finally bound or healed, slaves never fully free, the union would not completely be reunified, or warring parties satisfyingly vindicated.

The modern prophets of pluralism like Protestant Reinhold Niebuhr and Catholic John Courtney Murray had to deal with the perduring conflict and evil that pervade the structures of existence. Murray could and did assert his view of final reality: religious pluralism, written into the human condition and thus a denier of simple wholeness, was "against the will of God." But what chance did such thinkers have against the monistic hungers existing behind a romantic civil religion that would mesh a complex people and minister to the wholeness-hunger that came with the chopped-up and chopping sects? Or against the new therapies that called themselves holistic and wholistic at once?

Realism leads one to see ironies in attempts to satisfy the hunger for wholeness. The "primitives" back in shtetls, ghettos, wards, or valleys, were not nobler or lesser breeds but mere inhabitors of a different culture. Since they knew what bewilderments surrounded the ghetto or shtetl, they had to choose to live within the walls to which they were confined by force or social necessity. Many a priest in an Italian city or a pastor in grandparents' Swiss village possessed books that told of differences called heresies in another city far away, or in the valley beyond the next mountain. This meant that their people were victims or beneficiaries of "pluralistic ignorance," which was imposed because no one ministered to their curiosity, no one decided it was best for them to be allured by alternatives across the fence or range.

A second irony: if anyone in a ghetto, ward, or valley did become exposed to alternatives, both social and psychological pressure led them to patterns of constriction. People made aware of alternatives were trained to reinforce the boundaries of their lives, not to breach the walls and let the new lures find a response in them. They were to stamp out the heretic through inquisition, or keep the innovator at bay.

When change did come and freedom *of* choice linked with freedom *for* choice—the modern condition—another irony was visible. The newly advertised solutions only added options to bewilder the people left behind. A book by Leslie J. Koslof dates from late in the "revolution of choice," 1978; *Wholistic Dimensions of Healing* lists 1164 at least partly competitive categories, each of them presumably designed to satisfy hunger for wholeness. "Quintessence Unlimited" vies on its pages with "Reflexology" which cheeks by the jowl of "Getting in Touch" and "Anthroposophy." They cancel out "Aeroion Therapy," "Holovita," and "Temperomondikula," "joint technique." Other books with other categories and purveyors of wholistic philosophy and technique are down the shelf from Koslof: the choice verges on the infinite. Outsiders to each technique become aware not of the wholeness which appeals to a person's sense of entitlement, but of the brokenness that belongs to their bewilderment. *Hyperion's* charge is not utterly foreign in America.

No matter what care the observer takes, an unwanted note of derision constantly threatens a description like this which intends to be empathic and pathetic. If we are serious, we all enter in to the plight of change. Those who are responsive or pastoral have special reasons to bracket their judgment in order to understand the American version of the search for innocence, simplicity, and whole-gulp-at-once salvation. They do well to study the healthy specimens, the children and saints, the artists and healers, who live in awareness of choice and incorporate it into their emerging simplicities. Maybe in such living examples there can be guides for others. The eponymic figure is one who gives his or her name to a discernment. Such persons reach horizons before others of us and serve us with the names they give: Erik Erikson's "identity," Robert Coles's "crisis," Dorothy Day's "bread," Martin Luther King's "dream."

The pastoral discerner learns that there are available tools and instruments for patient people or they help the restless learn patience. Modernity is not without compensations. Who really wants to go back, behind anesthesia and social security? And the discerner learns to reject the big answers. You cannot blame all alienation fashionably on capitalism or all schism on communist class revolution. Nor is the advertiser or the mass communicator simply the villain. The political left and right blame each other. Each in the final logic would overcome schism in the soul and the society—but at unwanted and inflated prices. Discernment calls for subtlety. The final mark of prophetic boldness is called criticism, the ability to make distinctions.

Realists welcome solid fare to match their hunger for wholeness. In a republic, there have been "better angels" and "mystic chords" coming together, moments when transcendent justice broke through enough to make more of the republic possible. There are today glimmers of overcoming wholeness-hunger in the meliorist measures that revolutionaries despise among labor movements, feminist forces, civil rights endeavors, for the binding of wounds, rallying for causes. All these signal a wholeness that was previously absent. Through voluntary networks people address victimage and through social programs at their best they reckon with root causes. One finds glimpses of wholeness in the promise of subcultures, such as churches, or philosophies and disciplines.

If these are harder to discern in America than in some cultures, the difficulty results from richness. The natural resources of the land were so ample that there always seemed to be enough to go around. All citizens had to do was tease with entitlement. The human mix was also rich. "There goes the neighborhood," Americans say, but just as often there have come along people who enlarge horizons, whose strangeness, once disturbing, helps save, dissenters who once subverted but who later provided orthodoxies, or the immigrants who infused freshness in stale communities.

The public church, working in the context of biblical witness, promotes a realism about limits along with a limitless dream and invites people to learn to live with what looks like contradictions between them. This church makes its way in the midst of alternatives that too often obscure the realism.

Thanks to its evangelical component, the public church is opened to but not given over entirely to the various Jesus and pentecostal movements that focus on "the experience," on the decisive choice that comes with being "Born Again." Left to itself this tendency comes in the form of a prejudice against all Christians who have not had the precise replication of these experiences and against all humans who are not close to them. The heaven-pointed finger with the "one way" sign can represent decisiveness and resolve, but until it is qualified it will be simplistic. The Jesus experience is not confined to the "simple Jesus" of the "simple Gospel." Here the more complex side of evangelicalism and the Catholic and mainline voices insist on tentacles and connections in the Gospel. If "all things" cohere in Christ, as Paul says they do in the Letter to the Colossians, then one cannot hold to "one book" faith. "All things" are yours, says Paul, but "you are Christ's and Christ is God's." Savoring "all things," the believer connects with what is in the curriculum and the phone book, the library and the catalog—and reaches into mysteries undreamed of by the simplists. "Born Again" persons never deny the validity of their experiences and have something to impart to Catholic colleagues, but these in turn can ask, "What are you doing the rest of your life?" and answering their own question with the language of nurture and development.

Catholicism, where it reminisces in pre-Vatican II language about the "changeless rock" or relishes the selective authoritarianism of Pope John Paul II, can use the papacy and the magisterium just as some evangelicals can use biblical inerrancy: to give the impression that conversion or participation settles everything in life. Here the mainline Protestant voice, compromised as it is by its brush with relativism, is the intruder and questioning critic: Have you, dear colleagues, noticed what such authority does *not* solve? Catholicism has internal diversity and delights in a mystery that the teaching magisterium does not dispel and does not seek to. And those Protestants who agree on inerrancy are as diverse as those who cling to other versions of biblical authority. Invoking authority settles something, but it also leaves much open. Some years ago after Detroit turned "economy cars" into gadget-filled luxuries, it was said that this change "proved that Americans wanted economy and would pay any price for it." Such energies and investments come to mind as one watches those who want the tent of authority to simplify life, but engage in great complexity and intricate reasoning to keep it anchored and to help it cover what it was intended to. Finally even the tent-pitchers have to note that it was intended to cover a highly diverse congregation.

The third constituency of the public church, the highly exposed mainline Protestant cluster, is not an "anything goes" but instead is a "more things go" entity. So by definition it wishes to be open to a different breed of simplisms. When the counterculture of the 1960s pointed to the Native American world as being importable, the mainline sector became the advertiser of nature and tribe and their virtues. But soon it became evident that Indian religion was not so easily transportable, nor ever so neatly packaged. Was it simple? One book on the Sun Dance uses a computer to calculate thousands of variations in one dance among a few tribes. Anthropologists who are expert on the Zuni refuse to comment on the Hopi: it would take a lifetime to learn the ritual intricacies.

Africanity, the ethos of black religion, was supposed to be transferable from the black to the white sectors of mainline Protestantism. Its "primal vision" would undercut institutionalism and denominationalism, said the agents of transfer. But then black scholars spoke up, reminding the smugglers that Africa was not a glob, a simply outlined world, but a continent of nations, histories, tribes, visions, and contending realities. Mainliners gullibly imported Eastern religions to suffuse their practical-minded faiths, only to have serious gurus protest. "You should have eaten rice for a thousand years. You are too hasty, too simple about Oriental simplicity." And so it was with poetic Transcendentalism, the Thoreauesque "Simplify! Simplify!" or the fashionable therapies that were to provide direction for the mainline. Meanwhile evangelical and many kinds of Catholic Christians, serenely ignoring or disdaining the attempts to graft anything on to Christianity, served as judges or critics of the protean Protestant temptations.

Minorities in all three orbits of the public church for a time advocated modern communes or covenanted communities as ways of retreating from the world of computers and time-clocks. The models took the forms of simple movements like the Shakers of the nineteenth century, the makers of simple song and dance and furniture. Then they discovered whole libraries that pointed to discriminations within this one tiny moment, to tensions it was never able to resolve, to prices few then and almost no one now could pay to project such simplicity. The public church's current experiments: Reba Place, the Sojourners, charismatic communities, all may have validity, and they might embody new dreams for a timid time. But they also bring their own irony, for they demand great attention to intricacy and conflict, while people in ordinary communities are able to bracket some of these concerns and still to function in their callings.

All the sectors of the public church note the beckonings of political rightist and leftist simplisms that would minister to the hunger for wholeness. In Cuddihy's language, ideology is defined as the de-modernizing, dedifferentiating fabric. Formally, it makes little difference whether the total "if only . . ." solution turns out to be socialist or fascist. The public church does not suppress its elements when they advocate prophetic idealism in ways that overarch or undercut politics. But it is constituted in such a way that these voices have to counter more political and thus, in their view, more tainted and tainting questioners.

So we are all tied up in knots labeled complexity. Dreams end with cold-water wake-up alarms. Experiment is interesting but futile. Is that the message of the interactive and open church? Not quite. This church draws on a biblical charter that sees the people perishing without a vision—such as one which will lead to their return from spiritual homelessness. But when the promise of visionaries is too clean and clear, this church borrows Jeremiah's suspicious word-for-the-Lord and asks whether these prophets and diviners do not really offer false dreams. Tempering their call is the true prophet's mundane assignment: "Build houses and live in them; plant gardens and eat their produce. Take wives and have sons and daughters; take wives for your sons and give your daughters in marriage, that they may bear sons and daughters; multiply there, and do not decrease." And if that vocational commitment sounds holy and unstained, a next word in Jeremiah sounds as realistic as does the sociobiology of the selfish gene: "But seek the welfare of the city where I have sent you into exile, . . . for in its welfare you will find your welfare." Where in all this is altruism, self-sacrifice, or the intrinsic value of doing good?

Such an approach is not easy to market. One might almost invent a law of history, at least modern and American history: in any open contest, unless there are compensating factors, the less ambiguous vision, though false, will be more immediately attractive than the one that demands patience or allows for doubt and "on the other hands." It will also be more likely to have been found dangerous or wrong tomorrow, but today is the day when its attractions outbid the competitors. Religion has to come on with all the decisiveness of the dice-toss at Las Vegas or the coin-toss in the National Football League. The object falls one way or the other, so the God behind it must be decisive. One's club finds people either in or out. The book of spiritual directions has precise engineering solutions, with none of the doubleness that humans have to live with. A generation is untrained to look for something different in spirituality than in engineering, where things in the end always work, or in advertising, where promises always look true.

Perhaps the discussion of choice has sounded too remote and impersonal. What resources does the public church have for something less abstract than choice, more intimate like the journey of life of its members?

The public church, we said, is a communion of communions, a family of apostolic churches. But these communities and churches are made up of persons whose pilgrimages determine the character of the public church. If such a church community is a Christian form designed as a set of "little platoons" against Leviathan, against impersonal giantism, its leaders would serve no one well if they forgot its personal makeup and goals. Yet the pilgrimage within this church takes on a different spirit than would one in totalist religious organization. There, all steps are prescribed and only the subversive souls keep their quiet independence. The tribalist pattern is also easier because it is so prescriptive. It creates a tight family or protective cocoon in which all needs are met and all impulses toward deviation are prohibited. And the privatist mode of organizing religious life, while strenuous, is still easier because the consumer is in command and can freely and utterly pick and choose among alternatives that he or she finds agreeable. Because of the clarity and ease with which those three forms pattern life, they receive most attention. The journey of participants in the public church has gone neglected because its steps are subtle, the mapping is less well defined.

These participants—members at least, and disciples at best, but all partakers of the life in the body of Christ—have as urgent private and intimate needs as do those whose religious life is marked by unconcern for the public order. Somewhere along the way in the life of young persons, it dawns on them that they are somewhere well into the course of what Erik Erikson has called their one and only irreplaceable life script. The plot is underway, and they are in it. They can make changes within it, but they cannot get out of it. Being young, they find the choices open to them, yet these are ever narrowing.

If their nurture is in the evangelical tradition, it is likely that parents first dedicated them to God or caring adults sent them to Sunday School. Somewhere along the way they began to grasp, however dimly, a story that they felt had not reached all parts of their lives. The reader of a thousand Born Again autobiographies knows what to expect next. The young persons chronicle their wanderings: into religious apathy, waywardness, or delinquency. In the nurtured tellings, they then get sent to a Baptist summer camp or they come with a friend to a revival. In the more disruptive patterns, they become slaves of addiction or crime, and then a friend reaches out with an invitation. They situate themselves where a word of divine judgment reaches them.

At this point, the evangelical third of the public church has a distinct advantage, an advantage born of psychological quirks that have to do with modernity and that help account for evangelical appeals to the young. Anthropologists like Victor Turner have observed a widespread if not universal human impulse to associate an ordeal with initiation, in the form of familiar "rites of passage." The initiates move from a society which offered them a set of props and pass alone through an ordeal and over a threshold, until they are reabsorbed into a social form Turner calls *communitas*. For this reason, Born Again people tend to exaggerate, or at least to see their own story in most dramatic terms. Never was there a greater sinner. Never was one more abandoned. Never has anyone had a greater enlightening and awakening experience than have I when I made my decision for Christ, when he came into my life and I surrendered while he took over. I am Born Again.

Mainline Protestant and Catholic young people also may enjoy something sudden like a Born Again experience. Half of all American Protestants, when coached by a questioner, and a third of American Catholics, when the term comes up by an interviewer, will say that they have had an intensifying and converting experience that they call Born Again. Some of their response may be born of cultural fashion, some from the favor that having a new term for an old experience may supply, and most because great numbers of modern Christians have been always able to include conversion, awakening, revival, renewal, or enlightenment among their "varieties of religious experience." But in these sectors of the public church, there is less conscious programming for an experience that, if programmed, might violate the assumptions of gentler nurture.

Thus where infants are baptized, as they are in all of Catholicism and very much of mainline Protestantism, there may now also be a cherishing of a "second baptism" or "the experience of the Holy Spirit," especially since around 1960 when these churches began to be part of the pentecostal or charismatic movement. In other circles there was an affirming of baptism, a making one's own of a covenant once spoken for by others but not felt, in the form of confirmation. For just as many more, the movement to conscious adult participation is made by passage along a path of a million particular steps, not by a single jump.

So in this journey there come signals of transcendence, as Peter Berger calls them: clues that there is a sacred zone. Perhaps they become present because of laughter or hope, altruism or friendship, fear or mystery, or the first stirrings of basic trust. Then comes hesitation. Most forces in the culture around will deny the subtlety of these stirrings and bid one to escape, into hedonism, consumerism, or activist distraction. Television knows nothing of this journey on its main channels at prime time, and the evangelizers' own TV channels come from an arcane and, to the people we are talking about, charmless world. Public education largely screens it all out. The fact of pluralism means that most friends will not share the same language and cannot be reinforcers of one on the journey.

Yet, astonishingly, in many people the stirrings persist, and the young generation that was once distanced from the parental world, now begins critically to reappropriate it. Sometimes with a vengeance: younger people want to discern mystical traces and primal myths behind the serene and scrubbed facades of polite church religion. For some—up to forty percent of all Americans, though who knows how many because of mixed marriages—the turning may mean a change of denominations. Most stay within their own. But they will not do so unreflectively. The unreflective simply drift away, and have done so by the millions. So have some of the thoughtful who found nothing to help them along the pilgrimage. This loneliness is of the character of modernity, since religion or its particular forms has become escapable. A person sets out on a journey or follows trajectory. If the parental or some other accessible church provides a congenial climate for pursuing the already chosen, the young will follow. If not, they will go elsewhere.

Why? Sociologist Talcott Parsons wrote that persons in culture cannot let things "just happen." They must endow their fortunes and misfortunes, their joys and their sorrows, with meaning. As anthropologist Clifford Geertz defines the impulse: they have to keep chaos at a distance. Religious symbols and experience provide ordering against chaos and meaning where it had been absent. But in homogeneous cultures where one symbol-system alone was present, the search moved people with confidence over firm ground. Today the trip occurs, as it were, on the high wire. The strivers want and get a high-intensity experience, the only kind that will compensate for the lures of chaos. They are very busy, balancing, compensating, and gasping as the novice with a balance bar on the high wire must. And for all the lures of the experience, they will insist on a strong net of authority to break any possible falls. The cult leaders, the sectarian prophets, and the belligerent evangelists will provide this authority by claiming sacred *gnosis*, infallibility or inerrancy for their authority. But the public church, alert to pluralism, cannot and will not provide that form of authority, even though it is present in the repositories of evangelicalism and Catholicism. The special interiority of those traditions is matched not by complete closure, as it is in fundamentalism, but by specific openness, which carries its own but perhaps less question-begging authority.

Yet the stirrings remain. If these do not come with sudden intensity, then they do by quiet calls. The young persons suspend their disbelief not in religion itself—that was never at stake—but in the life world of the generation before them, the institutions that they felt never mediated well enough the message or way of life. Perhaps they can think of no single datable day of conversion; they were never *not* Christians, so how could they become Christians on a single day? Or they believed that they must become Christian everyday by affirming their new life in Christ. They follow this with a second recognition: as humans and as Christians, to be is to be with, *esse est coesse, Sein ist Mitsein.* They finally come to regard communal participation not as arbitrary and accidental and certainly not as a crutch for support, but as a special calling. The worship, the classes, the causes, the cells—all these become the stages for this life they hold in common.

They wish that the change in life *had* been more dramatic. All that happens among the Born Again nags them, too: it is easier to advertise conversion and to chatter about the experience than it is to *be* the new person of changed character. They read the biographies of heroes and saints and find the same to be true of these antecedents: all of them hope at best for a growth in grace.

The language of the journey remains appropriate, even though it threatens to turn to cliché in the public church. The participants need such an image to distinguish their way from the forms of Christian life which nestle people in cocoons. In those more sheltered forms one never, after coming to faith, appraises positives in the secular order or other religions, and becomes interested in comparable Christian communities only where they agree completely with what one already holds, nowhere else. The metaphor of the journey is as old as Abraham and Moses, as vivid as Jesus moving through the wilderness and from the mountain to Jerusalem. It evokes exodus and exile, neither of which were low-risk and protective forms of experience. In the journey, as the mystic Meister Eckhart put it, there is no stopping place, nor was there ever: there is always, even on familiar paths, only the new.

In the public church the participants do not turn their backs on supplementary signals. The people on the journey welcome the help they need wherever they can get it. A black like Martin Luther King appropriated nonviolence from Gandhi and Hinduism without losing Jesus. A Catholic like Thomas Merton reached to Eastern monasticism and mysticism without foregoing his hold to the center in Christ. Mainline Protestants live with what Karl Rahner called a "wintry kind of spirituality" as they reach for affirmations near the cold heart of secular and doubting moderns, only to take these yeses along with those anchored in Christian response already. These believers do not move off with some of their own kind to turn each of these open systems into enclosing ones. They let African or Asian spirituality suffuse their own without burning it away. In all these ways they revitalize their own culture and dispel the potential boredom with the merely familiar that would otherwise threaten them.

Along the way they have participated in a cultural recovery of the sacred, which is merely historically interesting, along with a personal exposure to it, which is existentially crucial for them. The experience takes differing forms in differing subcultures. Thus Daniel Bell thinks that evangelicalism appeals to a "moralistic" subculture that needs everything regulated by norm. The Catholic and mainline people he sees in a "redemptive" line in which they reappropriate a tradition. And the extremely high-intensity "mystical" types will go off to the cults which offer a total enveloping experience that cuts them off from public influences from without.

The assets of this spiritual journey are rich. Whoever has had such experiences will say they are of intrinsic value, part of what enhances human life, as valued as bread or Bach—more valued than both, because one does not live by bread or beauty alone. And they are integral to Christian formation. The Bible and the tradition picture, demand, and promise them to lean and hungry souls. Added to this argument for the intrinsic value is the evidential sign: some characters are changed and improved through it. Not always will this be apparent. When novelist Evelyn Waugh was converted to Catholicism he did not turn into a very appealing human being. Asked by critics what kind of an advertisement for faith he was, he wanted them to note that, however despicable he seemed, they should try to imagine what he knew about himself: how much more abominable he would be *without* Christian faith. There may be better advertisements than he for the faith: people less repressed, more open, more generous, more ready to take their weakness and doubt and let themselves be transformed into someone better.

Christians in the public church also remain wary of some forms of the journey. Its accent on self-awareness can mean that the believers remain in classic terms for sin, "curved in upon themselves." During the 1970s it was easy to show that cultural narcissism had found a cousin in spiritual narcissism. Self-engrossed people cared only for their own spiritual kick or high, and they became virtuosos at nuancing it in their tell-all autobiographies. They announced that they were "into" a progression of intensities, and they often merely dabbled and sampled the recipes of experience, whether as Born Again or in therapies. Often this all left them with a partial vision of the life of faith, which found them saying "Lord, Lord," without being or doing what life in the kingdom commits them to.

So with the turn to the new decade there came calls for believers to reconnect the inward journey of the seventies to the inward/outward course that the next generation in the rest of the century and millennium demanded. This combined course is one for which the public church claims to be adept at calling people, since it implies stewardship of the earth and a search for better social forms. It calls them to move on from mere personal experience to become again a thinking community, one that does not evade the issues of emerging science, literature, and social life.

Yet the spiritual journey is part of the mission of pilgrims in the public church. There, people will openly recognize that wholeness is a problem of community, that it is addressable but not fully soluble there or elsewhere. The free community cannot finally settle for either the demodernizing or the ultramodernizing situations. Demodernizing means that the community coerces assent and offers single, whole solutions. Ultramodernizing means that life fragments people by seeing them follow their impulses into utterly private solutions that *seem* to be whole because no one in the range of common commitment questions them. The public church critically appreciates modernity because it stresses free choice, but presents the vision of wholeness that keeps it from simple fragmentation. Brokenness and wholeness, complexity and simplicity, pure hunger and total fullness, each pair can tyrannize with their false alternatives.

Psychological reasons make the combination of inward journey and public call difficult to propagate, but there are theological reasons to promote it. What if the public church accepts the call to help people of biblical faith to rediscover these two poles of existence, and then to use them to inform life in a time when "the stakes are raised on both sides"? If this church succeeds, its participants would see the beginning of an epochal shift in Western sensibility. If it only partially succeeds, it will minister counter to the totalist and tribalist impulses which threaten the human future.

Participants in movements that might prefigure or induce such a change are invited not to an arrival but only to a journey. That summary sounds like clichés. It slides right past the mind. But people who take time to observe and join step find that, enfleshed and embodied, the idea of the journey does point to promise.

The public church is not bereft of the presence of God simply because it does not always banner and trumpet "lo here!" or "lo there!" The God who empowers its respondents is active in Christianity beyond the public church's borders and in the world beyond the borders of the church. But this cluster of churches is a community of praise that recognizes divine power and presence. The public church is not mindless about the private quests, but it rather expensively calls people to "seek their welfare in the city" and to stimulate social or public morale to enhance individual morale. The public church does not listen only to people in its own rational or experiential wings—and all three components have both—but instead reaches again for the depths in which reason *and* affections, both honored, are grounded in Being, in God. And the public church does not lack precedent or models, for now as before there are people and clusters who profess to deal with the complex simplicity and broken wholeness which are the best combinations one can find inside history.

The public church, for all the human imagination it takes to sustain it, responds to what it hears as a divine call and promise, once more from the letter in Jeremiah 29: "For I know the plans I have for you, says the Lord, plans for welfare and not for evil, to give you a future and a hope. Then you will call upon me and come and pray to me, and I will hear you. You will seek me and find me; when you seek me with all your heart, I will be found by you."

3

The Mandate to Congregate

The public church is a communion of communions and these, in turn, are also communities of communities. Most participants would regard the local congregation to be the basic expression of Christian community. While efforts to establish an essential form of communal life for Christians everywhere may be futile and may limit imagination, *something like* the local assembly will remain fundamental. The public church properly develops other forms to enhance the local gatherings, but it is not likely to settle for less than these. These congregations will take on varied colorings in different times or cultures, but in every case they serve to perpetuate embodiment, which is essential in the whole church.

Shortly after mid-century, the congregation suffered eclipse during a moment when experimenters promoted larger forms of community. Seminarians who were entering office characteristically told poll-takers that they aspired to ministries in agencies that promised more power and drama than did the local church. If only they could be mass communicators, workers for government, ecumenical field workers, or representatives of secular community organizations, they might be nearer the utopia of which the young must dream: that they might almost singlehandedly reshape a world. At least they could thus join hands with other people who had immediate access to networks of power.

Where universal or cosmopolitan forms of ministry seemed beyond reach, lay and clerical leaders, still despairing over the local church, were determined to set up parallel agencies of any sort to replace them. For a certain period these took the form of metropolitan parishes, paracongregations, chaplaincies to ill-defined respondents, nomadic apartment ministries, rural retreat communities, intentional congregations, or similar elites. Most of them did serve and their survivors still do serve as parables or exemplars for the more mundane congregations that remained prevalent. When these innovations failed and died, few mourned them, though many should have. In any case, in the present unfolding of forms, these para-parishes do not flourish and do not seem to be on the verge of doing so. The vast majority of participants put their communal energies into some form of local congregation.

Today instead of being assaulted or displaced by larger forms or mirror-image communities, the congregation suffers chiefly from a challenge to the communal ideal itself. A negative impulse often lies behind such rejection, for the congregation is an institution and modern religion abhors organized religion. The spirit of William James, a pioneer in modernity, has made its way. For him, religion was only the moment of incandescent stirring in the soul of the individual, the isolated mystic or saint. When two people linked up and set out to embody a spiritual experience through two seconds of time, the character of religion, he thought, began to be compromised.

The attack on the congregation as institution came from many sources. During a period of youth revolt the change derived from a spirit of anti-institutionalism. The churches were perceived as part of the power structure. People invested in them. Believers settled congregational affairs more or less democratically, which meant that they took votes, or creatively dragged their feet if they disagreed with the orders of the bishop. And if there was democracy, it was said, there could be neither prophecy nor purity. Religious institutions stifled the spirit and played into the hands of other grasping establishments. They were boring and lifeless, dulling to the spirit of adventurers, clouders of vision, promoters of mediocrity. The fact that there was and remains much truth to all these criticisms ought to keep the partisans of the parish from becoming complacent. But anti-institutionalism and the crisis of legitimacy together did not account for the whole of the assault on the congregation.

Instead, agents of modernity, as we have noted, consider that a contradiction exists between the religious spirit and social form, *any* social form. They celebrate and make a virtue of "the pluralization of life worlds." These moderns despair of any possibility of bringing such diverse personal worlds into confluence for positive purposes. They carry the chopping up of life and choice to the final degree. Religion becomes "invisible," says Thomas Luckmann, a "private affair," something which is an accidental and quiet footnote to one's biography but not something of social significance. To sociologist

Bryan Wilson sacrality would be apparent only if a whole culture would live by a single set of sacred symbols. Subcommunities in a society do not count. So each individual who cares for the holy must be a steadfast eccentric who builds a private castle or fortress inside the mind. In the mental stronghold the last and only shrine survives, and from it individuals may draw strength, but they can never share this strength, only live off it.

The consequence of this tendency is a world in which there will be as many religions as there are people. I am told that if two people would set out to move chess pieces through all the variations that the first eleven moves on each side allow, the possibilities would be nearly infinite. "If all the people now alive had been playing a game every few minutes since Christ was born . . .", they would not have exhausted these possibilities. Employing that sort of mathematics, one can imagine the varieties of, say, eleven component "private religions."

The pilgrim begins with recall of a Catholic childhood in the lower years of parochial school. But then mother remarried a Baptist, who would have nothing of such schooling. At summer camp, the child converts, is born again. Something of this second experience lasts. A high school girl friend who is taken up with the Transcendentalists comes along and under her influence, by junior year he is an ex-Catholic, partly Baptist, full time Thoreauvian. At college a Jewish girl friend appears, and while their tie does not lead to a permanent bond, she promotes a linkage to Hasidism. She also introduces him to I Ching and Tarot cards, which are "big at her house." He next gets into drugs and tries some peyote smuggled from the Native American Church. Then it becomes the hour for the counterculture, so he becomes a part-time and would-be Indian.

Nothing lasts forever. He heads back to the college community, where in the classroom he studies Islam and at the edge of the campus is "into" karma. The people he hangs out with belong to a commune which makes much of macrobiotics; you might say their diet is their religion and becomes his. To be neat in accounting for an eleventh ingredient—he never leaves any of them wholly behind—he takes a Master of Business Administration degree, marries an Episcopalian, and, liking the liturgy, joins but does not attend her church. This walking embodiment of modern religion, who displays differentiated, specialized, universal, diffuse faith, is never likely to find anyone with the same layerings or the same package. He is religious entirely on his own. *People* magazine and other monitors of the culture, when they discover him reaching celebrity status ("Recent MBA Invents New Economic Curve"), applaud the way he does not need institutional religion. The churchly alumni association gets the applause, never the strugglers with the curriculum and discipline of the church.

The members of the alumni association do not suffer neglect. They lack social power to effect change, but they do represent personal power since they are consumers who are attractive to purveyors. Unorganized, they are not in a position to inconvenience or save anyone, but they are poised to be approached with therapies or items of consumption. No one can ask them to "bear one another's burdens and so fulfill the law of Christ." But they can hear the burden of the television evangelist who needs money from them so he can reach someone in the next apartment, someone who hearer number one will never meet, need, or help.

These assaults on congregating from the side of private or custom-made religion obscure two realities: the congregation and the whole catholic church. Let me produce a scale to show which modes of organization do come more easily, in order to demonstrate the jeopardy that modernity creates for the local church. For reasons that I do not understand but which I do not find embarrassing, these fall into line under one letter of the alphabet, a mnemonic c.

First and most attractive is the *consumer*. The consumer remains free to buy or reject, to possess and to use, to cycle and recycle. Religion is something the consumers ingest or digest, one of the accoutrements to which they are entitled along with a vacation with Club Méditerraneé or a good evening at a singles bar. Of course, religious choice is more serious than these pick-up-and-drop elements of hedonism, but there is no essential difference between them. The consumer pays and receives for services rendered or goods acquired. There may be a spiritual high, an experience of healing, a moment of therapy, or an outlook that will produce more friends or more goods.

Second in complexity is the *clientele*. A clientele gathers around a charismatic individual or a celebrity who provides people with an identity or with services for specific purposes and during specific periods of time. A perception of this first social form of private faith occurred to me during a time of association with Irving Zaretsky, an expert of The Spiritualist Church. How many members, I asked, did it have? He answered: very few. It had only a clientele. People who wished to consult the minister, a medium, brought a question. She would answer it as part of the Spiritualist Church worship. If the answer was satisfying, the client would return—only good futures were welcomed. If the answer was not satisfying, the client must search for a new medium next week. Neither Zaretsky nor I would want to exhaust the communal realities of the Spiritualists with that observation, but it is sufficiently accurate to serve as a model of the new mode of spiritual attachments in America.

Millions of Americans today retain reminiscent or nominal ties to a church body and may on occasion attend a local gathering. But their loyalties focus on a celebrity who holds their attention. Editors of denominational magazines can certify that their writers can criticize popes, bishops, presidents, and pastors of their own church and meet little response. But if a magazine writer speaks critically of a currently popular healer, mass media evangelist, or author of a bestseller, the clientele will rise to instant and noisy defense. The celebrity, who is only "famous for being famous," knows how to use the media to enliven and equip such a clientele. In the Christian circle, such leaders use, and may well believe, words of the Christian message, which provide them an orthodox line of defense. To attack them seems then to be an attack on Jesus Christ. They are usually equally adept at conveying the idea that if attacks come, these issue from conspirators in the name of the devil or secular humanism. But the clientele is fickle, as the celebrities on the ash heap know: next year someone more gifted, more sensational, more attractive and promising may appear.

The fact that a large number of defenders of a single celebrity may appear suggests a third level of organization: *the convergence.* The convergers are not members of anything, except insofar as wearing a button or carrying a card from their celebrity makes them such. They do not relate to each other directly, but only through that celebrity who mediates their relations. Thus a typical you and I may never meet and would not like each other if we did. We have different styles of friendship, incompatible schedules and hobbies, courses of life that are complete on their own. But a Scientific Creationist reaches us both with a mailing that alleges that the theory of evolution is being taught as a doctrine in public school textbooks. Will we converge enough to send post cards of enlistment, letters of protest to school officials, and pledges to make our bodies available at a rally at the state legislature? So we converge on the cause and, after winning or losing it or until we are attracted by another one, move on.

Within clienteles and convergences there are some people who become personally acquainted with the leader. They take early retirement in order to move to where his studio-congregation gathers, or to the mountain retreat where initiates concentrate. They form a *coterie.* Picture life in it. We learn a language that holds us to the leader as the magnet. He is our guru, or she is our healer. We receive therapy from them. Sometimes a group process or a class brings us together into what passes for intimacy. But the communal experience is usually of a simple and straight practical character. If we wish to be near the leader, we have to be near others magnetized by him or her. We know what we want: identification, identity, *gnosis*. We take these where we can get them.

Next in line comes the *caucus*, a natural form because it relies on accidents of birth. As youth in a certain age-cohort, aged in another, or as women, as members of a minority group, as disabled or congenitally limited we gather. What we have in common on the positive side may be little, but we share more negatively. Middle-aged, male, people in majority groups, will overlook our interest if we do not organize to speak up for ourselves. Beyond our common feature in the caucus, we go our own way.

The *cult* is like a coterie, but is much more totalist in its makeup. The cult or intense closed religious group is born of a sense of anomaly. In it, the typical "I" must come to understand why there are Unidentified Flying Objects and then follow a leader who tells me that they are chariots of the gods. I do not follow the leader because I am open to a new approach to refugees, world relief, ecology, or revolution. I care only to make sense of UFOs. Or I want to know why as a black I am on the short end of history and how to get on the long end of its boons. So I join the cult of Father Divine and turn over to him the decisions of my life. The coterie allows its members some privacy, while the cult dominates, asks all, yields all, and creates a family.

Then comes the *cause*, which displays some features of the convergence and the caucus, but it takes more the form of a movement. The cause needs a more encompassing ideology and looks less "natural." Its members come with the conviction that no accident of birth or race put them in it, but rather that some moral choice, some gift of insight, unites the agents of the cause. Charismatic leaders may come and go but the idea of the cause perpetuates itself.

Finally, there comes the half-congregation or the *congregation*. To be fair, one can discern traces of all previous elements also in it. People inherit or retain life in a congregation because of the way it ministers to needs. Congregants are thus somehow consumers. When there is especially dramatic pastoral leadership or effective programming, a congregation shows similarities to a clientele, although this is a marginal and temporary feature. There can be common action in congregations as in convergences, caucuses, or causes. Sometimes elites within them form coteries. In some extremely close and semidetached churches which are remote from ties to other congregations, there may even be visible cultic features.

Over against all these, however, the congregation makes a virtue of the necessity of its accidents. More than one would wish in North America, people of one particular place do tend to be of a single economic group. Often the inherited congregational core—two-thirds of American Christians do not ever switch denominations—live in old mental furnished apartments and possess some common creed or treasure of hymns to go along with familiar smells and gestures. But the congregation asks its participants to be more than mere consumers, to overcome their instincts to be private religionists. They do not find the local church to be the crutch for weak faith, as the mass media often picture it. Instead, it becomes an arena for testing faith and thus improving inside the only kind of community one is likely to realize: partial, broken, unfinished, sometimes impetuous and sometimes ignoring. The local church is to be an invitation to people to share power, to multiply their efforts for work in the world.

All of this so far appeared in the language of social forms. We have not yet encountered the church as a community of faith, a theological reality. To make the shift to interpretation, I reach for extreme language from the early work of Dietrich Bonhoeffer, the German church leader who fell victim to Nazism. He was always concerned with the forms of resistance that a Confessing Church could make through its witness against totalitarianism. Never unaware of the power that one heroic individual can wield through gestures against the regime, he was more alert to the spiritual power of the conspiracy, which means people who "breathe together," in the community or congregation. In his early book, Bonhoeffer came up with a formula that has good New Testament warrant: *Jesus Christ exists as community.* At an extreme moment the theologian said, with the seriousness of sanctified gallows humor, that whoever in Germany did not belong to the Confessing Church was beyond the circle of salvation. In other moods, Bonhoeffer had to know that God did not necessarily ratify all the Confessing Church's decisions. But this was a way of expressing in shocking terms the moral fault that came along with the failure to be counted against Hitler and the deniers. He was also implying an extremity of statement: that Christ does not exist except as community or congregation. But is this so far-fetched? One can be a Platonist and celebrate the *idea* of Christ, or a humanist and welcome the *ideals* of Christ. But the participant in the body and blood of Christ is in the congregation where people recognize the presence of God and Christ is the sign of the New Creation.

I am not bold or brash enough as an interpreter to insist that Jesus Christ does not exist except as congregation. Too many secondary theological issues get piled on to make such an assertion simply stick. But if a person takes seriously the biblical witness to Christ's being the head of a body of the faithful, then to see the faithful choosing to sever from congregation is to expect a survival that the New Testament does not picture. There are and there may be legitimate Christologies of pure transcendence. Creeds and hymns offer imageries of Christic independence: "he sitteth on the right hand of the father." Why disturb them? Pull at one strand in Christian testimony and others can be skewed. So a sense of modesty leads to retreat from the most violent statements connecting Christ and congregation.

There are other reasons than modesty to inspire recognition of private witness. I have known Christian artists who made gifts of genius to the church while seeming to remain marginal to its weekly congregating. Something in their spirit churned with the motion of a divine torment that verged on the demonic, for the creative urge has its negative underside. Now and then such artists take part in the eucharist, the Lord's Supper, and they are bonded with those around them. But there seems to be no constitutional possibility for them to rein themselves in for modes of worship which dull them. The same may be true of all believers in some communities where congregating never seems vital, but that is a separate bane and to enlarge on it here will certainly disrupt our argument at this point. Similarly, there are the creative misfits in the church who take on the risks of distancing themselves and, as an act of judgment, will have little or nothing to do with congregating. In their view, the local church is nothing but the generator of "the noise of solemn assemblies." In cases where Christian heroism is evident, few of us have credentials to judge such a decision. But it is possible to say that with those decisions there must be compensatory commitments which are at least as strenuous as those in congregational life. These sometimes appear in the circles of critics or prophets who care enough about the church to spend their life fighting its mediocrities.

These artists and prophets, with their inner torments, are in a *caste* of reflective Christians alongside the congregation. I like to think of them incorporating themselves by the fire of their vision and the fury of their sense of justice, or being incorporated through the prayers of contemplatives who keep the whole interests of the church in mind. In this company, of course, one also thinks of those shut in by disease or shut out by a petty church: they live off the congregating of others and live with a less visible form of communion.

Those of us fortunate enough to belong to promising liturgical fellowships, to hear evangelical preaching, and to be confronted with lively programs in local congregations, are tempted to be unsympathetic when someone comes along from a community where none of these are available. Go down the street to another congregation? The street is long, the place is lonely, and not for many miles is there a gathering of promise. And what happens to the idea of "local" if one shops too far? The advice is valid: be sure that your standards are not such that no existing fellowship anywhere can be shaped in accord with them. But a frequent response is, "Come along and see what I mean." One comes. One sees. Eventually counsels of despair are in order: you can think your own thoughts through the worst of sermons; do your own applying of the text. But what if there *is* no text, and the sermonic book review of the week is so distracting that I cannot even locate my private thoughts in the word of God? Then make the most of the great language of hymn and prayer. But, comes another reply, we don't come within *miles* of great hymns and prayers. So, plunge into the acts of mercy and justice to which congregations are committed. But, we next hear, the church I should be a part of denies every chance to be converted to such commitment. In such encounters we smile knowing but sad smiles at each other, and drift apart. We congregators have no easy answers then.

These exceptions, no matter how vivid or massive they may be, do not detract from the image of God present in the congregation, of Christ existing as a community. Hans Küng addresses this theme: "The Church begins, not with a pious individual, but with God. The pious individual cannot by himself achieve the transformation of isolated sinful men into the people of God. How could an atomised crowd of pious individuals be a home for the homeless and isolated men of today?" The church of which Küng speaks is not simply the congregation. It is also other than and more than the local assembly. But it is not less than such a gathering of participants.

In the primal documents that lie behind the life of the public church the social and communal dimensions are prime no matter what cultural shifts occur. Creation is a social act. God engages in an act of process by forming responsive universes, worlds, and humans. Creation establishes communion. The fall, that great mystery, is a corporate act. Whether the fall transmits itself through history, ontological fault, or broken personal responsibility, it is somehow corporate. The divine address to the fall is the promise of a people. Its first prefigurement is the *Qahal Yahweh*, the congregation of Yahweh. "Once you were not a people, but now you are a people."

In the covenant in Christ, which is grafted to the original one, the plan remains one of congregants. The choice by Jesus of The Twelve replicates and affirms the tribes of Israel. A new covenant associates the old promise with the new people. Here imagery and reality of

Christ as head of a body is in place. The New Testament knows of no consumerist or clientele religion, but always it is the congregation that seeks to transcend caucuses of male and female, causes of bond and free, or coteries of Jew and Greek.

To justify the congregation in the networks of the public church is not to settle all the issues of its function and mission. The local church too is a community of communities that, whether small or large, may show some temptations to totalism or may splinter into private interests. For that reason some experimentors have seen it as a cluster of ever-shifting intentional subcommittees. Professor Carl Dudley argues that a church with fewer than 200 members might still be seen as a "single cell," and in many circumstances that could be an apt model. But in larger congregations these subcommittees, never elites, seek to enlist people of various talents for temporally limited commitments. Some of these devote themselves to addressing the problem of drug addiction, the possibilities of the aged, the clarity of worship, witness through the arts, community change, and the like. Members of each of these find themselves so charged with meaning and burdened with work that they seek and need the gathering of the larger fellowship. With their bodies, presence, prayers, and notices they enliven others or unburden themselves in the gathering of the congregation.

This is not the place to prescribe congregational life but only to describe the status and locale of such community in the public church. Each church will need to discern its own genius: what is distinctive about its confession in its place? It will have to be inviting and invitatory. If people do not sense the presence of God in worship, they will not respond to calls to service. The congregation does not stand alone. It is not a microcosm of all that the church in the world should be. Locale has limits. Though a local church can be an agent for stimulating the imagination about congregations and individuals in other circumstances, it can become self-enclosed. The best chance for revitalization occurs if the local community conceives of itself as a way station between the encompassing world and the private individual, between the church catholic and faith in solitude. Then it can find its rightful place not as an end in itself but for people on their journey.

Part Two

Movements within the Public Church

4

Prophecy and Politics

The public church as a communion of communions is, when viewed from some aspects, a political church. As political, it includes elements of compromise. When compromising, this church will strike some critics as being unfaithful. And if unfaithful, its very existence has to be questioned.

In modern North American churchly conflict, four models compete. One is the totalist church with its autocratic character. Someone decides issues between parties, and that settles that. At the opposite end is the familial church, which is necessarily small or cohesive. Many of the ethnic bodies in America were once of this sort. They lived as primary associations, where people could be accountable to each other. Ordinarily these were paternalistic. The father or bishop decided what was best. But the attractions of membership were so strong that few bothered to question his decisions.

When the familial model breaks down, two options remain, though in practice one of these, the military, predominates. The military mode is much like the totalist, except that in its case a party that rises in defense of a doctrine or a practice gains and wields power against other parties. Whether originally a minority or a majority, this force becomes ready to use any instrument of power so that it can prevail. Usually its leaders make demands for unconditional surrender or drive their opponents into exile, as military campaigns are wont to do. Because they fight for an abstract ideal—in Christianity today it will be the tradition, inerrancy, or infallibility—they can look as if they transcend personality conflicts, and thus can make their causes appear noble. But this quasi-military way of resolving conflict has taken a fearful toll, and thoughtful people seek a fourth alternative.

That leaves the political mode which needs a good word of defense. We have established that the public church includes mainline Protestants, evangelicals, and Catholics whose communities are open to each other. Openness does not mean that they agree with each other in detail. Suppose that many Catholics emphasize papal infallibility, as they are almost certain to do during the reign of Pope John Paul II, and thus, following actuarial prospects, possibly through the rest of the second Christian millennium. While Catholics hungry for authority may relish the assertion of infallibility, non-Roman Catholics show no sign of being able in good faith to accept the dogma behind it. Similarly, to deny papal authority would be to threaten the Catholic community as now constituted. Basic principles are at stake.

Within Protestantism, most people called evangelical insist on a Born Again experience as an adult, usually datable, always intense personal decision to accept Christ. This turning is not universal. Evangelical parties in Lutheranism and Anglicanism have never spoken in these terms. But in our culture the term "Born Again" attaches itself congenially to the evangelical parties. Meanwhile the Catholic elements in mainline Protestantism baptize infants. While they may or may not confirm young people who were baptized as infants, they do not attach to confirmation the values of initiation and decision that evangelicals do to conversion. Erosion of distinctions between these two parties are not much more likely than they are between Roman and non-Roman lines of authority. For the immediate future few envision a way to overcome the difference.

A loss of integrity would result if any of the three components pretended away the significance of their separate stances. Yet some sort of compromise is necessary if they wish to remain a communion of communions. Compromise cannot mean that Protestants come to believe that the pope is two-thirds infallible, or that Catholics must mean that they can give up one-third of their belief in papal authority. Infant baptizers cannot compromise by half immersing semi-adults, and adult initiators would not make sense if they made similar concessions. Compromise has to mean finding patterns of coexistence and common action without a loss of integrity on other levels in the fundamental patterns of church life.

The picture so far is too simple. Each of the three major complexes of the public church is itself a community of communities. In Catholicism the names for these communities might be Benedictine, Jesuit, Italian, Third World, charismatic. In the two Protestant clusters the community may include communities of Presbyterians, pentecostals, conservatives, experimenters, and various sorts of movements. Whoever has seen any of these up close knows that they too are rooted in conflicts of wills that force some sorts of political accommodations.

Coexistence is very unsatisfying to the purist. Once upon a time purists, who look for community without compromise in response to the prophetic word, experienced little troubling of mind in respect to the church's integrity. They would not learn about lapses until centuries later, when historians revealed from the archives the frailties and concessions of long-dead pontiffs and pastors. Today purists are sophisticated as they pursue their suspicions, so they know at once when integrity is at issue.

This sophistication comes along with the general growth of public suspicion. Economist Kenneth Boulding has for some years been pointing to the "decay of legitimacy" as a problem for all public institutions. None are exempt from the charge that they are self-seeking power structures, worthy of being dismissed. Attacks fall on government, politics, business, the military, the university, and the church alike. Mass media have helped generate suspicion, since they accent vivid and conflictual, not serene and secure aspects of institutional life. And they do so instantly, and from great distances. Believers formerly might have had to live with the scandal of compromise in their own church but once in a lifetime. Now the reports on one summer's worth of church conventions can lead to an erosion of confidence in the integrity of the church conventional. The tape recorder of the FBI prevents moderns from joining the ranks of the equally frail saints who preceded them.

Alongside the opportunities media provide for generating suspicion a new awareness of human fallibility came with the collapse of humanistic optimism. Dr. Karl Menninger wrote *Whatever Became of Sin?* long after awareness of fallibility increased. Street wisdom confirms what formal theological and psychological analysis reveals. Celebrities "tell all" to publics in frank televised autobiographies. Revelation of lapses in integrity in the bedrooms and the legal dealings of the stars help elevate the audience by cutting heroes to size. Many of these heroes and heroines have been celebrated church people, and they have cut themselves to size.

Suspicion directed against the church is not new but now it is better focused. I have often stood before a large black sculpture of the god Horus, as found in Egypt and refurbished by the Oriental Institute at The University of Chicago. The caption tells gazers that the beak of Horus once moved. Through the carved body ran a passage for strings which the priest behind the scenes could manipulate. The faithful thought that they were talking to an unseen spirit. Instead they were in conversation with a ventriloquist's dummy. That deception is just the beginning, thinks the skeptic who pursues Horus through the ages—down to *est* and scientology, the Worldwide Church of God and the Unification Church, the Pallottine and Pauline Fathers, and all the other groups that remain in the news because former followers or publics point to alleged rip-off artists in their leadership. The higher the stakes the more gullible people seem, so religious forces can best exploit gullibility, and the suspicious will know it.

Meanwhile, a sacred aura that once surrounded inherited religious institutions has tended to vanish. Less social distance remains between participants and leaders. "Nothing is sacred" in a voluntary society where the buyer bewares and chooses a belief, thus remaining in command. During the competition, entrepreneurs overreach and underachieve, so they have to make their next act more sensational than their last. The public watches. Marxist and other radical critics have decided that the church is a prime agent of repression based on duplicity, and they too have provided publics with instruments of attack on churchly forms. Where there are partisan disputes, each side lets the world know through the press of the evils of the other. A Christian "prochoice" partisan lets one know that antiabortionists inhibit freedom while "antiabortion" camps call their Christian counterparts murderers, in what are not the gentlest of attacks on integrity.

Add to all these the purist or rigorist attack on the integrity of churchly institutions. All three of the main component communities have generated creative in-house critics. Lacking personal qualifications to be prophets, in most cases, they hold up the standards that are to measure the churches, and are easily able to show them all wanting. For some the very institutionalization of religion is itself an act of political compromise. In some cases, critics do bring prophetic credentials and risk everything for their vision. In other cases, they band together and overlook the fact that thereby they too become institutions. In both cases, so far as the outsider is concerend, attacks on compromise are consistent and telling.

In all instances, the key item under scrutiny is Christian integrity. Integrity should belong intrinsically to churchly intentions. As Adlai Stevenson used to say of earthly politics, "No one runs on a campaign program for corruption." People who claim to be following the God of truth recognize that integrity must be a prime mark of the church as it pursues its goals. Integrity is also a mandate to the believers: "Be ye perfect." The Sermon on the Mount, seen as part of the original charter, allows for no compromise of integrity, no qualifications on the purity of followership.

Integrity, Christians say, is not only a goal but also a gift to the church, to be expanded while it is being cherished. The church is and seeks to be an extension of the body of Christ and derives its qualities from the degree to which it is found to be "in Christ." But it is one thing for an individual to accept the gift and another thing for a diverse church, where conflicts of wills among the *symbiotes* issue in negative actions toward one another. They are struggling with truth and for appropriate patterns of action, and they meet opposition within. All churches do this, but the public church is open about this dimension of its character.

Being public about the need to bring discordant wills together is not the same as letting go of the quest for integrity and prophetic clarity. The church is the community of those who are hearers of the word of God, custodians of its seriousness. This community does not hear the word in the form of God proposing a notion for seconding and debate. But it does hear that word in a complex world of difficult choices, and the listening ears belong to people who hear its meaning for them in diverse ways.

So it is that someone in the public church hears and applies a controversial word. For example, one subcommunity decides that American churches must disinvest themselves of property in South Africa in order to advance the cause of racial justice there. But another concludes that disinvestment is not favored by all blacks, who would be put out of work or who fear immediate violent revolution. For another example, among the evangelicals one cluster has "the experience," recognizes a second baptism, and insists that all people in Christ must speak in tongues. Another finds the experience permissible and plausible but does not prescribe it. Again, one evangelical says that the inerrancy of the Bible extends to its geographical statements. But another contends that the infallibility of the Bible points to the fact that it has its own integrity and displays utter faithfulness while mediating the truth of God for faith. Finally, one Roman Catholic believes that the church is indefectible and that in its overall thrust it will not permanently fall from the truth, while another contends that the pope is infallible and should assert his own authority as often and as vigorously as possible.

Does integrity demand that each of the sides in these sample polarities must break relations with the other? In some cases they will do so. The inerrancy faction is likely to force out more open evangelicalism, and the papal infallibilist party will remain at a distance from the seeker for parallel bases of churchly authority. But even in matters of social policy or less definable personal experience, some will insist that coexistence with other *symbiotes* amounts to taint in the short pull and a denial of truth over the long haul. They may recognize that total agreement among humans is never possible, and will hope not to be pushed to define too clearly where the points of fellowship must constrict their own faction of factions. So before the question is even brought up, they move into constricted Christian patterns, away from the larger community of communities.

Most contending parties do stay. Is this because their ministerial minority would be inconvenienced by a change in pension plans, or because they want to avoid a messy fight over the division of church property? Are those who stay merely the weary, those who care less about truth? Or could it be that these have thought through the character of humanity and history, including the limits of redeemed humanity; that they are aware of how God works in the brokenness of history—riding the lame horse, carving the rotten wood, as Luther would say—and so they do not expect a realm of pure prophecy in the world?

They well know what happens in the loss of devotion to truth. Augustine wrote: "When regard for truth has been broken down or even slightly weakened, *all* things will remain doubtful." They know what happens with the loss of integrity. All of us are acquainted with people who are aware that we know that they know they have "sold out." They keep up appearances, and their facade is marked by a devil-may-care grimace. But somehow they are enthralled by the inroad that the lie or false compromise has made on their integrity. They must look at those to whom they have lied or whom they have betrayed with a new caution. Will the knower not think that a web of duplicity is now being spun? After the first threads, the others come more freely, until the seller-out knows that nothing is left to compromise. The value of a word given as a pledge declines, and the level of trust falls with it.

The public church also includes many who have taken the measure of politics in social forms and have sneered at its claims. Of course, social life includes clash of wills. Of course, no set of wills can always be right or always get all it wants. Of course, retaining of community will often call for some yielding, some settling for less than purity, less than the arrogant claim that one always knows the truth and acts in accord with the will of God.

The lie, it has been said, has one face, but truth has many. In her uncompromising book against *Lying*, Sissela Bok quotes German theologian Dietrich Bonhoeffer, who owned credentials on both sides of the issue. He was insistent on the integrity of the church. When the Confessing Church was born to oppose Hitler while others in the established church sold out to him, Bonhoeffer, as we have seen, sounded extremist and said in effect that outside the Confessing Church there was no salvation. All others lacked integrity. Yet this same Bonhoeffer worked through the church with duplicity and high-risk compromise in the effort to bring down Hitler and end the Nazi tyranny. Bonhoeffer said, "It is only the cynic who claims 'to speak the truth' at all times, and in all places to tell all men in the same way but who, in fact, develops nothing but a lifeless image of the truth. He dons the halo of the fanatical devotee of truth who can make no allowances for human weaknesses; but, in fact, he is destroying the living truth between men. He wounds, shames, desecrates mystery, breaks confidence, betrays the community in which he lives."

In other words, truth breaks through human personality. It is embodied in fallible people who coexist and support one another in community. On such terms, we shall survey some of the types of instances in which, it is said, people compromise integrity in the life of the church.

Every element in the public church has for a century been going through a crisis of interpretation. Their actions provide a first illustration. The historian is aware that never has the church known a fully settled period. The earliest church, as reflected in the Book of Acts and the Pauline letters, was full of tumult. Parties had to coexist and compromise for the sake of truth personified. The transit, begun in the New Testament, between the church as an emphasis within Judaism and thus in the Hebraic thought world and the church as an agent of thought and action in the Roman Empire and the Greek thought world, consumed three centuries. Residues of the conflict and compromise live on in the church into the present. In the thirteenth century, the thought of Aristotle, remote as it was from the Christian types of theism, reached the West through the instruments of the infidel Muslim. But a new generation of scholars addressed the challenge and used its pattern to formulate a Catholic orthodoxy that has lasted for centuries. There were fierce factions within both the communities of Protestant interpreters and Catholic counterreformers. Many Catholic bishops called the dogma of infallibility "inopportune" or opposed it and absented themselves from Rome in 1870. Only the uninformed think there was no clash of wills or doctrines within the constituent sectors of the church throughout history.

The modern assault on inherited thought patterns has been especially challenging to the integrity of church teaching and practice. New instruments for interpreting sacred texts arrived in the same century that saw the rise of the theory of evolution. The eighteenth-century Enlightenment and the nineteenth-century encounter with world religions led many to see a relativizing of Christian truth. Some believers, in an expansive and protean spirit, simply embraced the new ideas and were dissolved in the new world. As believers, they disappeared with hardly a trace. Others froze their understanding, developed closed and constrictive personalities, or thought they could stay above the battle by trying to be apart from it. Yet even the most resistant enemies of modernity found themselves changed through encounter with it. The rigid doctrines of scriptural authority in fundamentalism are inconceivable without the rise of certain schools of early modern philosophy like Baconianism and Scottish Common Sense Realism. Militants who opposed the Darwinian theory of evolution adopted its general scheme in their economic outlook, their social programs, and even in their tests of truth ("the survival of the fittest") in competitive church life.

Yet among the open-ended components of the public church, there have been pioneers called to be on the spot in the issue of integrity and compromise. These are literary figures, artists, theologians, and experimenters with churchly forms who have a vocation to express and interpret the faith, to discover and inquire how it may speak to people in new worlds of thought. Chroniclers of modern church history have seen in this community many people of true integrity who wrestle with conscience and understanding. As innovators they know that they must win some battles and lose others. As explorers, they follow blind leads alongside appropriate ones. Following their maps, they develop some languages and concerns of their own that are not immediately translatable to the whole body of the faithful.

From time to time, one or another of these stumbles across an insight that may eventually enlighten but will temporarily disturb the church. The people who hold the new view believe it to be a clarifier of faith. But it appears to be different from the majority view. Should they voice it? To do so prematurely makes them look like destroyers in the eyes of those who can not or will not understand their mission. Some of them lose heart and disappear, or become vocal in defense and are put out of respectable church circles. Should they be tentative and rather quiet about their vision, instead? To do so makes them look like subverters and conspirators in the eyes of those who stand ready to pounce on them in their midpassage. So they are vulnerable. Exploiters make them seem duplicitous. Meanwhile the encrusted church, content to have pleased itself by growing a thicker shell, is convinced that it has pleased God by keeping it.

In the early 1950s *Look* magazine once bannered on its cover that the New Testament has something like 150,000 errors. The faithful rose up in perplexity or anger. In response, thousands of preachers had to get up and painfully explain what "textual criticism" of the Bible means. This form of criticism has been safe in the bosom of even the most conservative church bodies for a century. The article was enlarging upon the fact that the ancient manuscripts have thousands of conflicts with one another. The ministers could say that they were familiar with these from the footnotes to the Greek New Testament which their most safe and scrupulous seminary professors had mediated to them. None of the variations challenged a basic teaching. Only a few cherished passages were called into question: the ending of Mark's Gospel, a story of a woman taken in adultery, the end of the Lord's Prayer, a passage in a Johannine letter. But among thoughtful people the damage had been done. Why, they protested, did you not have the integrity to tell us years before about the unsettled character of the manuscripts? Why did you wait until public embarrassment forced you out into the open? What else are you holding back? Yet if these leaders *had* made textual criticism a topic point in their educational ministry, their enemies would have hounded them for having weakened faith, as if faith depended upon the absence of variations in the manuscripts.

What else are you holding back? The community of scholars takes for granted other kinds of biblical analysis but is not free to mediate them because exploiters of churchly unrest will challenge their integrity. As a result, lay people—lay so far as scholarship is concerned—are deprived of the opportunity to examine views that the discoverers find to be, at the same time, threatening, exhilarating, and capable of goading them to better understandings of the original texts. The public church is learning that there must be room for artists to breathe. Literary figures and scholars in their experiments must be given the chance to be wrong, just as they need to learn that they may be guilty of misleading sometimes, when they are called to lead.

Failure to understand that some forms of political compromise do not compromise integrity has consequence in the ploys of church power. After years of debate on an issue, a majority at a convention finally prevails. For example, a church that once did not ordain women votes to do so. Opponents feel left behind by the changes that led to the policy. They do not necessarily believe that the church has simply turned false and now denies Christian truth. But they cannot personally do an about-face. They cannot rewrite the tradition. Such opponents do not find themselves convinced by the arguments adduced by the time of the vote. Then it is that the majority is tempted to turn triumphant and, in the interest of celebrating victory or avoiding untidiness, they try to enforce their new way on tender consciences or clouded minds. Whereupon two integrities clash. The one insists on the validity of whatever the church passes, and the other on retaining a policy long cherished. Since politics involves give and take, winners find it hard to give and are unwilling to live with a generation of possible unsettlement. The creativity of conflict disappears the morning after a convention resolution, and all parties lose.

Changes in rites or retentions of old ones, another controversial instance, admittedly belong to the political life of the public church. Thus when the Second Vatican Council prescribed mass in the language of the people, it did not say that people for hundreds of years were wrong or misguided when they used Latin alone. This means that the integrity of neither the old nor the new forms of the church was at stake. Nor did the bishops claim that their predecessors had been wrong when they insisted on meatless Fridays or on certain acts of piety that the postconciliar church no longer prescribed. When they moved the altar so that the minister began to say mass facing the people, they made no judgment that for centuries priests had been wrong in their postures. But the spirit of the enforcer tempted some of the changers. The innovators often unthinkingly imposed the new order over the old. The official Roman Catholic church unquestionably had the power to act as it did, but this power often came unmediated by a sensitivity that would have looked like compromise to the reforming purist.

To criticize the enforcers does not imply that truth comes "down the middle" through the search for a golden mean in church conventions. Moderators or ameliorators do not replace prophets. Keeping the community together is not the highest value. Nor does such criticism mean that churches must avoid controversial opinions so that conflict has no chance to appear. The church is not only a forum but also a voice. But there are issues in which no clear word of truth emerges. Components of the church from congregations to ecumenical conclaves can often yield without abandoning conviction on profound subjects of debate.

Yielding is creative when all sides understand that all institutions are political. Even a form as intimate as marriage gives expression to two wills. At least two people's set of interest needs representing. Marriage can be autocratic or couples can live on the principle of mutuality. All organizations are potently political when they subject issues to vote. The fact that an issue is legitimated in the assembly by its placement on an agenda implies a political understanding. When antiabortion elements ask people in their church to vote on their issue, they have to be ready for no votes. If not, they should never have asked. What is definitely determined in the voting is not the truth of God but the convictions of participants, fallible as they are.

Certain strategies serve to protect the integrity of the church. Not all compromise compromises integrity. Many decisions are no more important than selecting a door knob for an assembly room or choosing who will repair a lawn mower. Somewhere on a scale of issues people have to be vulnerable to defeat. Second, respect for the integrity of the defeated commits those who summoned the most votes to reincorporate the losers. On the other hand, the defeated are not free to exercise a tyranny of their own as the walking wounded, the outnumbered but still visible virtuosos of noncompromise in a world of phonies. Further, the public church has to learn to do what its ancestors did: to live by the centuries. A generation heals wounds after conflicts which no one during the intense moments could settle or live with easily. Someone within or outside each party has to call victors into judgment by reminding them of the fallibilities of majorities through the years. They have as often as not been wrong, and historical review can show how they have been wrong.

When something like compromise is called for close up to conscience, a group of Christians may have to invoke an "ethic of distress" and assert the prophetic word against the larger body. When such prophets have sufficient perspective on themselves to live with a sense of humor and an ability to prick their own pretensions, healing comes quicker. And in times when compromises are less expensive, all elements of the public church learn the benefits of meliorism. The church Catholic is by definition internally diverse and, within wide but defined bounds, inclusive. The church evangelical lives by a pithy Gospel that does not establish answers to all questions of human policy. The mainline cluster is a group of survivors who have built in both adaptation and prophecy.

In the New Testament Paul spoke for his own integrity during mainline, evangelical, and Catholic church disputes in Galatians. The account of these by a church historian in the Book of Acts has a different tone and emphasis. Paul is all passion and furious integrity. His opponents in the church, he thought, were going to change the basic character of the faith. Paul had found his calling as an apostle to the Gentiles in an act we often call his conversion. Perhaps it should be celebrated as the apostle's vocation day, for he did not even switch denominations. At the time, his choice was whether to remain a Pharisaic Jew or a Jesus-following Jew, and that choice meant a call to carry the message to the uncircumcised. Paul's subsequent stand was not a focused dismissal of Judaism, which in Romans (Chaps.

9–11) he clearly showed belonged in the covenant. His attack was on Judaizing *Christians,* who would pervert the character of the good news.

The rage of a man fighting for integrity crisps the pages: "I am astonished that you are so quickly deserting him who called you in the grace of Christ and turning to a different gospel. . . . There are some who trouble you and want to pervert the gospel of Christ. . . . If any one is . . . let him be accursed. . . . In what I am writing to you, before God, I do not lie! . . . But when [Peter] came to Antioch I opposed him to his face, because he stood condemned. . . . O foolish Galatians! Who has bewitched you? . . ." The church of later centuries would be poorer apart from the Pauline defense of Gentile freedom, stated here without compromise.

The historian of Luke-Acts, however, has a different view and intention. He is writing much later, providing a story to keep the church together while the wounds of conflict still throbbed. His voice of compromise still charms. Acts 15 says that "some men came down from Judea and were teaching the brethren 'Unless you are circumcised according to the custom of Moses, you cannot be saved!' " Even in this elegant and smoothed version, the passions are visible: there was "no small dissension and debate with" these "some men," now conveniently unnamed. Paul and Barnabas, on their way toward participation in the brouhaha, get credit for spreading "great joy." They were "welcomed" by the church that Paul insists he stood off and told off. But some partisans still insisted on circumcision. "Much debate" followed. Now Peter, seen as a prime antagonist in Paul's account, becomes the seeker of a third way. He and Paul, in this synthesis, came to an agreement on the deepest issue, that neither circumcision nor uncircumcision saved, but "that we [the circumcised] shall be saved through the grace of the Lord Jesus, just as they [the uncircumcised] will."

The keeper of the minutes of the meeting years later has Paul and Barnabas state the radical case. Following it came four delightful phrases: "It seemed good to the apostles and the elders" to select apostles and send them out. Actions came before the words that would follow in an accompanying letter. Then, "it seemed good to us in assembly" to send out others to settle unsettled minds. The third time the phrase grows longer to legitimate the compromise. Neither side should have too great a burden laid upon it. The legalists would not insist on circumcision and the Pauline party should be respectful of their sensibilities by "abstain[ing] from what has been sacrificed to idols and from blood and from what is strangled and from unchastity." Given the earlier stakes in the game, all this was easy. The legitimating phrase sneaks in and with its subtlety stuns: the first compromise "seemed good to the Holy Spirit and to us."

The prophets and purists may sneer that Acts needs to report on the Holy Spirit only in the fourth and most delicate point. But the church lived with this compromise after the time of "no small dissension and debate." The Lukan mellowness which complements the Pauline fury has played its part in keeping the church alive for the staging of later, equally fateful, summonings of conscience. The spirit that seeks the good of the Christian *polis*, the city or community of communities, has not always been prophetistic. Not always was it given over to the shrillness of those who always have to be uncompromisingly right.

Or so, at least, "it seemed . . . to the Holy Spirit and to us."

5

Unity and Mission

The church grows by spawning new generations of believers or winning newcomers through a set of activities code-named evangelism. The constituents of the public church bring a variety of complementary outlooks on evangelism to the present scene. The evangelical component is most adept at seeking to extend the reconciling circle. Evangelism is integral to evangelical self-understanding and programs. Great numbers of participants find it easy to witness to other people and to seek conversions. Many of them do this without creating the impression that theirs is a god of prey, who causes them to pounce on people. They have learned to respect the integrity and humane existence of people who do not believe as they do. Another element in the evangelical orbit displays a harder edge. Left to itself, it tends to value people only if they have been born again or if they are prospects for the evangelical recruiting experience. Interaction with mainline and Catholic Christians forces this wing to rethink some fundamental biblical motifs and to fashion varieties of ways to cooperate with those in the constituencies not dubbed evangelical.

Mainline Protestants pioneered in the ecumenical field, often at the expense of the evangelistic impulse that originally gave them life. The Episcopal and Lutheran constituencies, for some exceptional examples, never adopted revival techniques, though both include large evangelical wings and both have excelled in what was once called foreign missions. Meanwhile, in America at least, the heirs of Congregationalism, the Presbyterians, Methodists, Disciples of Christ, and northern Baptists, now all securely in the old mainline, did profit from the century of great revivals in Anglo-America after the 1730s. Like most religious movements, these were born of personal fervency that effervesced into clusters, congregations, and then great organized impulses. In American history the great evangelical revivalists, the Edwardses, Tennents, Finneys, Asburys, Stones, and Lelands—unremembered names in the larger culture now, but once towering in their times as Billy Graham does in our own—worked in the tradition now called mainline.

Late in the nineteenth century, thanks to the restless student movement, returning missionaries, and thoughtful laity, leaders in these churches got the message that the central Christian theme of oneness in Christ had been hopelessly compromised. Southern Baptist, northern Methodist, Norwegian Lutheran, and Scottish Presbyterian outposts and extensions had to contend with each other to establish clinics, schools, and churches on a typical Micronesian islet. In order to legitimate their competition for converts they had to stress their differences, not their likenesses. This meant also that they had to engage in unbecoming and, they came to feel, unChristian boasting about their own superiorities. They began to play a game born of the Enlightenment, in which people did not ask what it meant to respond to the concrete call of the Christ who stood in their way with a mandate and an invitation. They indulged, instead, in a kind of "my God is better than your God" taunting spirit.

So it was that by 1910 at an International Missionary Conference at Edinburgh they began to charter an ecumenical movement that came to a crest with the formation of the World Council of Churches in 1948, a subsequent National Council of Churches in the United States, and a number of federations and mergers in many parts of the world. During some of those years, the evangelizing impulse began to wane. This change came about as a result of confrontations with the other religions of the world. The superiority game made no sense in their presence. Some relativising and loss of nerve led others to forget their grandparentage in schools of personal witness. Exposed to the larger culture, many mainline Protestant Christians began to be embarrassed over the idea of speaking up and trying to persuade anyone else to believe as they did.

Some cynics eventually saw the ecumenical movement as a ploy by dwindling churches to gain power while cutting their losses. Others argued that the loss of the evangelizing impetus was a direct result of their ecumenism. By 1970 a new law of history was developing. If you wish to evangelize, you must be cocksure, absolutist, unfriendly to other Christians, rejective of humane values outside the community of faith, and a bit pesty if not belligerent as a personality. To be ecumenical meant to be half believers, certainly nonevangelizers. If that law reflects the true picture to any extent at all, the mainline needs evangelicals to get back in touch with its own roots so that its participants can make more intelligent decisions about the future.

Meanwhile, Roman Catholicism retains long ties to evangelistic and missionary movements. In the time of the Catholic Reformation, Jesuits like Francis Xavier set out to evangelize the world. From his day until now missionary orders have extended the Catholic faith into the Western hemisphere. Recent studies by Notre Dame historian Jay Dolan and others have revealed that nineteenth-century American Catholic revivalists borrowed from Protestants or, on their own, developed techiques of revivalism. In any book of world history, Catholicism has to look like an exclusive and expansionist faith.

Despite this history, and despite its record of growth in mid-twentieth-century America, Catholicism has become relatively inert as an evangelizing force. The church developed its own cynics. "If you can't convert them, conceive them," it was said of the era when Catholicism grew chiefly through efforts at growth through large families. Stringent requirements that someone marrying a Roman Catholic was to bring up the children Catholic led to many conversions at the time of marriage. Then, decline in family size and slight relaxation of the marital requirements after the Second Vatican Council cut into the pattern of growth on which the church had relied. The typical North American Catholic was unwilling, unready, and unable to speak up for the faith and commend it to others. The Council permitted Catholics to enter the era of open ecumenical ties to mainline Protestants and evangelicals, but it issues no compensatory evangelizing momentum. Later in the 1970s, with their ecumenical outlook reasonably assured despite many continuing restrictions, Catholics began to look to the friendlier camps of evangelicals in order to establish their own priorities for connecting evangelizing and ecumenism.

To periodize the decades after mid-century: in the Fifties, mainline Protestants (and the Orthodox) got themselves together. Then came Vatican II, which eclipsed those efforts. A Consultation on Church Union had been developing to bring black Protestant and mainline Protestant bodies into a Church of Christ Uniting. But the new drama appeared on a different stage. So the Sixties were spent in efforts to get mainline Protestants, now gotten together on a certain plateau, into communication with Catholics. Once these two reached a certain level of detente, they began to reappraise their grasp of the whole Christian message. Both of them independently of each other and together began to relate to evangelicals. This symbiosis produced the emerging public church for the 1980s. But the efforts still left large questions concerning the interplay of evangelism and ecumenism. Top-level programmers and bureaucrats pursue them on one level, and all the participants in the public church pattern have to face them on another.

The themes are symbiotic. Ecumenism is a problem for evangelization and evangelization is a problem for ecumenism. The centrifugal and centripetal forces are in conflict. Since they are both rooted in the church's original hope, its present definition, and its outlook toward the final outcome, those who care for the church see them in a Whiteheadian projection: a clash of doctrines is an opportunity, not a disaster.

Ecumenism is a problem for evangelization. Yet the church never has a choice but to be ecumenical. To deny the task of recognizing unity is to obscure the Christ who is head of the church, his body. Coming to terms with that fact demands heroic intelligence and will in an age when interests of sociology and strategy both lead programmers to make it a secondary theme. The reader need scan no further than the first three chapters of I Corinthians to find an unmovable chunk of biblical lore around which evaders cannot detour. No paraphrase substitutes for quotation from those pages written by the apostle Paul to a factionalized church.

"I appeal to you, . . . by the name of our Lord Jesus Christ, that all of you agree and that there be no dissensions among you, but that you be united in the same mind and the same judgment." Paul had heard of quarreling among the participants. Participants had been negatively "denominationalized," so that some belonged to Paul, some to Apollos, some to Cephas, some to Christ. "Is Christ divided?"

Two chapters later Paul said of the church what has never been repealed: "For while there is jealousy and strife among you, are you not of the flesh, and behaving like ordinary [people]?" So long as there were these conflicting denominations named after Paul and Apollos, the Corinthians were "merely men," merely "of the flesh." So long as there was competition, there would be boasting. But "no one [should] boast of men," for "all things" were theirs, "whether Paul or Apollos or Cephas . . . all are yours; and you are Christ's; and Christ is God's." Later the church compromised away the brunt of such passages. Christians can gerrymander their ways around these by making psychological comments on the creativity of conflict and the variety denominationalizing brings. But before parties compromise, they have to hear a clear word about what they may be bartering away. A strategy for church growth which overlooks or denies words like these, or even stronger ones from the seventeenth chapter of the Fourth Gospel, moves on strategic, not truly evangelical bases.

Paul issues not one pragmatic or calculating word. He does not ask them to be ecumenical in order to get more members, just as he does not call for them to be less ecumenical in order to do so. Much legitimation for current church growth comes from economist Adam Smith's rational calculations about markets or Charles Darwin and his jungle in which the fittest struggle to survive and outlast the unfit. For Paul there is only a theological theme which might be called a higher pragmatism: be ecumenical, or that to which evangelizing is directed will not be the kind of community early Christianity envisioned.

To be bold about it, in biblical charters there is no church but the ecumenical church. To be anti- or un- or paraecumenical is, in the Pauline scheme, not to be of Christ's church. There is only one church in intention and as a goal, in Christian archaeology and eschatology. The communion has one head and is one body. Churches, from this point of view, are at best fractured members. Though still somehow attached, they are at their worst acting "according to the flesh."

In history, however, this church is visible only as a struggling force in a fallen, unfulfilled broken humanity. As such, what we see is a sign, not a completion. In Martin Luther's terms, this church is a *Werden,* not a *Sein,* a becoming and not a being. Mainline Protestants are tempted to make too much of their faithfulness to such a "processive" view of the church, one that is always in the process of becoming one. Their *symbiotes* from the evangelical flank can show that the mainline is equally adroit at neglecting the complementary mandate to extend the church. The self-critical evangelicals have data in hand to show that their colleagues, in their own turn, were often ecumenically faithless. Historians looking on the scene observe that evangelicals have learned more about ecumenism, both among themselves and with other Christians, in the past decade, than these other Christians have learned about evangelizing.

Evidence is stunning that the psychology of opposition to ecumenism breeds an impulse for aggressive recruitment to belligerent competitors. Why scholars have to ponder this is itself a puzzle worth pondering. If you believe that yours is the only boat that will reach the desired shore, that all others are half-safe or unsafe, and if you operate under a command or simply feel called to rescue those hanging to planks, you will do this more zealously and efficiently than if you feel that others are also valid. In the first picture, you may have great trouble understanding what the other vessels are for, or why God permits them to float and to delude others with the hint they may be safe. But you will be sure of efficiently taking stragglers in dark waters onto your own craft.

If you only have mandates to attract people, to compete for their loyalties, and to outdo others, you will excel in response. Psychology underscores this, though it has very little to do with the nature of the church as its charter documents picture it. When one component of the church follows these exclusive mandates, it will dismiss the other churches or see them as inferior. Sociologists parade knowledge of this tendency as a fresh discovery. It should have been obvious at least since Adam Smith and Charles Darwin, if not since chapter three of Genesis and the story of the Fall. What demands skills of discernment is to see how the competitive theme squares with the story of redeemed humanity.

All this is blunt and harsh language, biblically valid but historically unrealistic. I would qualify it by commenting on the term ecumenical which we splash so casually on pages like these.

Ecumenism, first of all, does not imply one strategy, form, or model for unity. The modern councils of semi-independent churches and the mergers of denominations are not prescribed in biblical charters, for the simple reason that such churches and clear-cut denominations had not yet arisen to create the problem for which they are partial solutions. We cannot take the Corinthian passages and say Apollos equals Presbyterian, Paul equals Baptist, Cephas equals Lutheran, and Christ equals ———— fill in the blank with the church of your choice. We can only say that men and women of imagination, in their desire to be faithful, invented these forms at a certain historical stage in a common quest.

The destinies of the public church in America, its components, and the world church are not tied to one passing form. Some day historians will look back and say, "Thus and thus is how people addressed this problem back in the twentieth century." By then other addresses will have been devised and outworn. The era from 1910 to the 1970s will be seen as an episode, no more. Its episodic aspect is clear from the patent signs of decay in the uniting patterns of the time. They were too much marked by what Max Weber called *Rationalität*, a form of rational bureaucratizing that was often remote from the life of ordinary participants in the church. As organizational ecumenism tried to give expression to voices from all over the world, its political aspects became ever more evident. The original dominant ecumenical form was too Euro-American. Subsequently, in encounters with the rest of the church Euro-American bodies, through their ecumenical leaders, often capitulated to national and social ideologies that were Asian or southern-hemispheric. These were simply different and possibly salutary, but not above politics.

As a result of many trends and forces, by the 1970s the mainstream ecumenical movement was in trouble, however healthy the ecumenical spirit remained. The crisis of legitimacy that afflicted most institutions hit the ecumenical forces hardest. People who were immeasurably closer to each other in Christ than they could have been were it not for the endeavors and successes of the pioneers, took these gains and gifts for granted. Without sending a card of thanks for their achievements, they yawned—or sneered.

The benefits of the twentieth-century unitive endeavors are obvious to those who take pains to reflect. Once upon a time a pioneering Denis de Rougemont had to say that he could not wait for the churches to recognize each other, so he had to create a one-person ecumenical movement. Later the movement in this episode turned churchly. In local communities there was evidence of new ease and warmth and a freedom for common tasks before remote higher jurisdictions had solved everything. Area, regional, and national churches found common cause before committees of hierarchs signed articles of agreement. On the highest levels, earnest committee people continued to make progress on issues that divided them. But taken together, they could not claim to have come up with the only model that fulfills biblical mandates and promises.

Just as ecumenism does not mean a single model for all time in the public church, so it does not demand the disappearance of lively diversity. Christians can take seriously the theological thrust of Paul writing to Corinthians without dropping their guard. Alert readers of the same documents will know that Paul lived with a broken church and that he contributed to the brokenness himself. The New Testament does not show early participants more united than modern historians find their successors. Yet the church functioned. Vital differences between the parties of Paul and Cephas outlasted their political efforts at compromise. Worship included a spectrum from uncontrollably charismatic outbursts in Corinth to more staid amens elsewhere. Sermons by Paul lasted so long that listeners fell asleep and fell in their sleep. Faithful probers of the early documents can find bases for congregational, presbyterian, episcopal, and hierarchical ways of governing the church. Theologies in Petrine, Pauline, and Johannine succession complemented each other or vied, with as much difference in world view as one finds today between empirical, idealistic, and existentialist schools. The New Testament letters and the Book of Acts depict vastly different strategies, to say nothing of

clashing personalities. Evangelizers often spent little energy trying
to exact expressions of unity. One thing at a time, seemed to be their
motto. We do not receive clear clues about the rites of passage that
are vital in Christianity as in all faiths. Did the early Christians baptize infants? They fought over the apportionment of charities. Yet all
this added up to the one church about which the various writers were
so firm and sure.

Given such circumstances, believers fairly ask whether diversity
cannot be a boon as well as a blight. The modern temptation is to
push the obvious yes to such a question to inordinate and even
dangerous limits. In the modern world the natural impulse is to
produce as many churches as there are individuals. As there is a
"pluralization of life worlds" in the surrounding milieu, these are
present also in the church. Because newcomers have so little in
common when they come to faith, there seems little value in advertising diversity at the expense of communion. Celebration of variety
takes on more, even problematic, tones when it merely represents
traditions as the decor of churchly life. My prayer book language has
to be preserved at all cost. Your style of architecture dulls the spirit.
When such aesthetic impulses come to dominate and push aside all
other questions, elements of diversity become idols.

Add to this an issue left over in evangelical church growth circles,
and another complication rises. Some experts, noting that people
best work for church growth with their own kind and that they want
to share intimate communion only with their own kind, have turned
their observations into an ideology and called it the Homogeneous
Unit Principle. Efforts to form local communities of faith, if they
follow anything but the lines of "our crowd," must be inefficient,
says this principle. Orientals want to worship with Orientals. Blacks
want to interact with blacks. Suburbanites do not care to worship
with innercity dwellers. Those in the $18,000 income bracket desire
congregational life with others in the same bracket. They "snob out"
or feel "snobbed out" by fellow worshipers in the $28,000 bracket.
This being the case, Christians should abandon the efforts to encourage internally diverse communities. They should reinforce and even
sing praises for the diversity of self-enclosed clusters of believers.

The Homogeneous Unit Principle, which confronts mainline Protestants and Catholics from the side of evangelicals, illustrates the
benefits of symbiosis. First it exposes them. Christians have long
cherished the notion that in all dimensions their churches were
catholic. Yet the H.U.P. promoters demonstrate that they almost
never are on the local level. In Roman Catholic circles, ethnicity

marks parishes that have little in common with those of other national backgrounds. Protestant congregations are so layered by their makeup in various economic classes that they show little empathy for people outside their own bracket. The Principle has been a great unmasker.

Second, this Principle, which issues from one of three clusters in the public church, is a strategic challenge. "Look, your units and ours *both* live by a homogeneous rule. But we at least make a virtue of this necessity and do something with it. We use it to help like convert like. We have brand names but we use them to sell the product. You have the same kind of units but you not only do not recognize it; you do not do *anything* with it. You are winning neither like nor unlike." Until that challenge begins to be met, apathetic Christians who profess to believe in evangelism have few credentials to judge those who bring the challenge.

To these we add a third moderating theme. Those who advocate the Principle do show some uneasiness with it. For example, they advertise some local congregations that in effect are made up of three or four churches. One is largely black, one Hispanic, one Angloid. Yet the three also stimulate interaction, perhaps by having one common building, a central governing board, and some common acts of worship. Where, it is asked, do you mainline Protestants and Catholics embody such models?

Finally, units of the Homogeneous Unit Principle can effectively keep alive legitimate bonds between tradition and faith. People are not believers in general any more than they are humans in general. Faith bonds with the senses. As philosopher Ernest Gellner says, "Traditional cultures smell." They may smell of incense or garlic, the must of sweeping compound in churches or the coffee pot perking during an overlong sermon before social hour. Faith, no matter what the purist says, comes as a package deal. It is part of a life that is fired point-blank at believers. I, for one, admit that a visit to a nearly empty sanctuary where an organist is practicing on a Saturday afternoon does more for building my faith than does reading systematic theology. If so, I am recognizing that faith comes along with connotations and supports. I will not nurture these elements if I am blurred and blended into a nondescript communion.

Having said all this, dangers are evident when planners shift from the Homogeneous Unit Observation to the Homogeneous Unit Principle. The particular, which should be one pole of Christian existence, ought to remain in tension with the universalizing impulse. Instead it takes over, and what was held in common disintegrates. The public church is a communion of communions, but all the energies go into the subcommunities. Over against this come words of judgment from biblical witness. Those who claim to be responsive to Paul's impulses recognize that his whole life was a breaking down of Homogeneous Unit Principles in congregational embodiments. His letters spent less energy on telling how people should get saved than they did on how diverse kinds of people, Jew and Gentile and so on, could live together within the congregations. To abandon the reconciling and transcending motifs on the local level would be to desert a uniting theme in the New Testament. So the Homogeneous Unit Principle is not something that the public church must reject but something that it qualifies.

The argument over that principle and its negative features distracted from what I intend to be a celebration of diversity. Ecumenism is not the suppression of diversity but the effort to share separate gifts, in local and larger contexts. It regards as assets the separate smells of traditional cultures, the differing sounds from organ to guitar in different cultures, and the differing theological tones of voice from one confessing body to another.

Just as one cannot impose a single ecumenical model or use ecumenism to suppress diversity, so, third, ecumenism does not mean the search for a power bloc. The public church as a community of communities builds in enough diversity to be able to resist temptations for Christians to unite for aggression. Yet as the communal spirit develops, such temptation grows. I recall sitting over coffee at little outdoor tables in the Via della Conciliazione during prolonged sessions of the Vatican Council. Often my company would be American Jews, who also were getting fatigue of the nerve endings after hearing several hours of Latin. We took refuge under the sun. One noon as a couple of thousand purple-clad bishops poured out of St. Peter's, a Jewish observer, Joseph Lichten, knowing my enthusiasm for Christian concord, asked, "Should we Jews hope you succeed?" Lichten knew that many efforts to unite had taken their drive from a spirit directed over against someone else, be they Jews, humanists, or infidels.

The current pattern of ecumenism shows few traces of such a spirit. Even those who once hoped that a uniting church would be a bulwark against atheistic communism were soon put off by Pope John's friendly spirit toward visitors from the USSR. Jews were not fully content with the Council formulae on Judaism, but these certainly moved the church further toward embrace of Jews in four years than nonecumenical Christianity had moved in four centuries. The council document *Nostra Aetate* demonstrated a positive appreciation of non-Christian faiths that had been unforeseeable for centuries. Other documents showed Catholics trying to understand, not to kill, unbelievers.

Lichten's question stung anyhow. Earlier stages of Protestant church union were often designed squarely to counter Catholic power. Catholicism sometimes suppressed internal ethnic and ideological diversities in order to create an impression of bloc power in American urban politics. More recently on the fundamentalist right many competitive leaders admit that they cannot overcome their differences over baptism, the millennium, or pentecostal expressions. Still, they plead over television, they must unite over against nonfundamentalists, liberals, and humanists, in a power struggle whose prize is America. The danger of negative coalition, then, is latent, but in the public church the grasp for monolithic bloc power is limited.

The ecumenical movement may have included goals of personal glory for leaders, bureaucratic rationality for its functionaries, and mindless glossing over of difficulties by the indifferent. But it also was and remains fundamentally a response to the Pauline question, "Is Christ divided?" When Christians were geographically remote from each other in the East and West, there was less urgency to answer. When Protestants and Catholics were geographically separated, there was less offense in division. But in the era of modern media and mobility, the scandal became more visible and the contagion to recognize and express unity spread.

The day of relative achievement eventually arrived. Once upon a time ecumenical leaders in their evangelistic spirit complained that their work was ineffective because people would not respond to "many Christs." Get your own act together first, they were told; stop competing with each other, and we will take you seriously, said outsiders. Later, church leaders discovered that there were now greater problems and scandals. A secular world found the Christian word to be arcane and pointless. A serious world found the messages and practices to be petty and trivial. A seeking world found Christian experience to be banal, seldom intense. Philosophers in search of meaning found the language of and reference to God meaningless. The ecumenical achievement then showed that Christians had taken a fundamental turn. When participants in one Christian community instinctively rejoiced in the victories of another, or when they inflexibly mourned in the trials of another, they "telegraphed their shots," and in doing so overcame the worst of the scandal.

By the last quarter of the twentieth century there was more frustration over lack of unitive fulfillment than there was rejection of the ecumenical impulse. The failure of Christians to be able to unite in the eucharist remained the single most troubling issue. But it was possible now for two-thirds of the public church to recognize a different set of needs and hungers. If to evangelize is legitimate, the Catholics and mainline Protestants began to learn a need to compensate and to engage anew in the act. To the cynics all this looks like an attempt to "play catch up ball." In this charge, the laggards have read the signs of the times and looked at evangelical adding machines in envy. Efforts at church growth then became a new if ineffective example of bureaucratic *Rationalität*. In an era of inflation, one hears, it is inefficient to let Christian communities get so small that they do not pay their own way. The list of taunts can grow to indefinite length. But mainline Protestants and Catholics have also, for a variety of more noble reasons, had to come to terms with the latent call to evangelize that gave birth to their own heritages. What are they doing with it now and what should they do? Have they distinctive versions of the task to bring as their gift to the public church and through it to the world?

Questions crowd to the mind. Can such communities make their shift without contributing to the growing religious intolerance, of which the world needs little more? Can they combine a new commitment to evangelism with an old practice of civility, which was so hard to learn and could now be so easy to forget? Will they become busy maintaining boundaries and building walls around their homogeneous units and will they then neglect their enlivening cores? Some present styles of growth seem to issue less from love of God than from despising others. Will they be able to pick up better models? Evangelism task forces show that such questions are alive. Therefore, just as ecumenism is a problem for evangelism, so evangelism is a problem for ecumenism. It poses issues similar to those in the civil order. How does one blend civility and commitment, and in ecumenism and evangelism, exactly to what is one committed?

Recent awakening to the need for evangelism by Catholic bishops and mainline Protestant leadership is a step in the recovery of something once strong and now almost forgotten. But the renewal is also a belated means of catching up to modernity. To some ears it will sound strange to hear that fundamentalists, evangelicals, and pentecostalists are the true modernizers in Western Christianity, but in this one respect at least this is true. Near the essence of the modern outlook in religion is the expression of choice. The mainline Protestants understood that fact back in the New England revivals of the 1740s and the early 1800s. Methodism had a virtual patent on that notion during its years of greatest expansion, late in the eighteenth and early nineteenth centuries. Catholic missionary orders knew it. But their followers established themselves on new turf, settled back, and forgot it.

Territorial Christianity, of which they were a part and which some of them still wish to exemplify, thought that Christianity was transmitted by law, turf, and bloodlines. By formal definition, to be a Jew is to be the child of a Jewish mother. As Edmund Morgan said of the elect Puritan people of New England, they thought that piety passed through the loins of godly parents to their children. Faith was a genetic transfer through the generations. Christianity did not derive from such a conception, for the simple reason that it builds upon rebirth. Unless one is born "from above," he or she cannot enter the kingdom. So deeply did the later cultural assumption win its way, however, that many non-Christians think it belongs integrally to the faith. The Jewish minority in North American or European culture considers those who are not Jewish, Muslim, Buddhist, Hindu, or whatever, to be Christian. Why? Because they are on Christian soil or had Christian grandparents. Mainline Christians who reluctantly supported the separation of church and state never quite got over the notion that faith came with the territory. But by the late twentieth century, as they watched their own new generations-by-blood disappear and never turn into generations-by-faith, they had to scramble back to their roots. In the process, they became part of a larger movement of people who were catching on to the principle of modernity.

Several examples illuminate the trends. In autumn, 1978, Reform Jewish rabbis, through the voice of Rabbi Alexander Schindler, came into the open to advocate Jewish efforts to convert others. A year later there appeared a book which effectively demonstrated that such efforts were integral to Judaism in earlier stages but were now long forgotten. Jews afflicted with amnesia about this history or eager to cultivate a myth suggested, contrary to all the evidence, that Jewish chosenness had always kept it from an impulse to gather others to it or to exact commitment to the synagogue among those born Jewish. After their devastating rejections in Christian cultures and with the rise of the ghetto, Jews could no longer expect conversions. Marginal Jews instead passed as non-Jews, thus entering the larger culture.

Three mid-twentieth-century events changed this picture. The Holocaust led to the loss of millions of Jewish lives and reduced the community of Jewish peoplehood. This forced on Judaism the issue of survival. Second, the rise of modern Israel provided Jews with new motives for surviving and a new focus for establishing identity.

But they found they had to make a case for Israel and must work to help assure its future after threatening wars. Third was the often overlooked element of suburbanization in America of the Jewish community after mid-century. While ghettos broke up and synagogues and self-help organizations lost some power, Jews moved next to non-Jews and found much of their community dissolving. New York City had 2.1 million Jews in 1957, 1.2 million in 1974, and 1 million in 1979. Most of them were unsynagogued. Young Jews provided cohorts for new intense religious groups which appealed to them during their search for identity and familiality. The Eastern communities like Hare Krishna recruited among them. "Jews for Jesus" raided them. "Mixed marriages" grew in number, and conversion outside Judaism further cut into the numbers. Following these trends, in a couple of generations there would be comparatively few Jews left.

So the rabbis openly advocated efforts to get Jews by blood to be Jews by faith, to turn Jewish peoplehood into Jewish practice and seek converts. "They won't get good at it," sneers the observer who sees the habit of recruiting atrophied. But even if the rabbinic urging looked like a counsel of despair, it represented a vivid awakening to the reality of modernity. And if the effort succeeds in gaining any numbers of affirming Jews at all, a generation will have felt it acted responsibly on its new realization.

Other religions of the world provide a second illustration. Islam, it must be said, like Judaism and Christianity, was born in an impulse to attract others by coercion or persuasion, but this motif was not visible in America until Black Muslims and more orthodox followers of Islam asserted themselves in the 1960s and 1970s. Non-Western faiths like Buddhism and Hinduism, for all their sectarianism, were not known for proselytizing off their turf. The pilgrim must find the guru in the Himalayas, must stare at the wall for years if so commanded, and should have eaten rice for a thousand years to become the good Hindu. But when modernity hit Hindu cultures and Hindu offshoots arrived in pluralistic environments like America, they had to turn "evangelistic." The Society for Krishna Consciousness and Transcendental Meditation were simply the best known among scores of efforts by participants to work campus areas, street corners, and airports, in quest of converts. Conscious efforts followed to cultivate celebrity converts, in order to give plausibility to recruitment. Gurus made well-publicized stops at airports, where metropolitan religion editors paid attention to them far beyond what the numbers of incense-bearing adherents who greeted them warranted. The gurus seemed to transcend the fuss, but they cleverly nurtured the publicity in efforts to attract more followers. Their successes among the Catholic, Jewish, and mainline Protestant young inspired counter-efforts.

Late-twentieth-century Roman Catholicism was a latecomer to evangelism. After *Nostra Aetate,* with the decline of missionary orders following Vatican II, and in an era of new friendliness to other faiths, the evangelizing impetus was dissipated. Catholics knew how to missionize populations better than individuals. When Christians converted King Clovis or turned Boniface and Patrick loose, they could bring a whole people to Christ. But they were at a loss to convert individuals on alien soil. By the middle of the twentieth century, to say that an American had converted to Catholicism usually meant that he or she had married a Catholic. At the same time, eloquent leaders like Bishop Fulton Sheen and Father John Ford began to attract celebrities and intellectuals like Clare Booth Luce and Thomas Merton. All this was seen as the expansion of an elite, not as systematic evangelization. Not until the period when the young drifted after Vatican II did the bishops begin to sound aggressive about the need to evangelize.

Mainline Protestantism, the quintessentially modern faith in other respects, was slow to catch on to the need for winning the loyalty of its own younger generations. It profited from an artificial and illusionary boom when ex-GIs and others planted roots in the suburbs in the 1950s. For a time, these went back to the most familiar if least demanding faith they knew for the sake of their identity and the future of their children. Then these churches languished. Their original progenitors, John Calvin, Martin Luther, Thomas Cranmer, John Knox, spoke from the first of a need to spread the Gospel, but few of them took pains to spread it beyond what they could have called their crowd. Lutheran pietism on the Continent, evangelical and Methodistic outbreaks in England and America, and the foreign mission movement after the 1790s engendered evangelizing activities. The groups that now make up the mainline therewith entered the modern world. Eventually they grew comfortable and forgot their origins. Evangelizing henceforth tended to be an act of renewal that came "from the fringes," as it were, in the evangelical camp, among pentecostalists and various Wesleyan offshoots through much of the first half of the twentieth century. Whether or not the mainline Protestants will adapt to the hunger for choice that is so visible among moderns, or will content themselves with forming task forces or evangelism committees, it is too soon to tell. Almost certainly, they will not get as good at attracting newcomers as evangelicals temporarily are because of the way they interpret their mission.

A half century ago, the mainline sector of the public church counted on numerous accessions from the camp of repressed fundamentalists. Once upon a time the fundamentalists did the converting. They thereupon allowed for so little development or freedom among the Born Again that many of their thoughtful young felt a need to escape. They sometimes reacted by adopting antichurch or non-Christian expressions. More often than not they "moved up" into the mainline bodies, where they displayed Christian loyalties but also enjoyed more freedoms. Several things have happened recently to cut off that flow. It is easier now to escape church religion into the zone of private faith or nonfaith. Young citizens gain little by way of respectability because they are church participants. Family and social pressures to conform have declined. When mainline churches grew too diffuse, they no longer served as magnets of loyalty. More important, evangelicalism, as it moved toward a new mainline alongside the old, offered more varieties than did its antecedents fifty years before. These generated their own freedoms and respectability. Alert observers could discern a trickle of members from revivalism toward higher-church Episcopalianism. Some former fundamentalist Campus Crusaders formed a body to express identity with ancient Catholic orthodoxy. Statistically these movements remained small. The mainline element knew it would have to do its own attracting and retaining. Hence, it readopted the language of evangelism.

I passed too rapidly before over the unacknowledged but strong rationales for conversion in the trail of modernity. Darwin, a symbolic name here, deserves more than the one-sentence mention. Some suggest that Christians must be absolutist, fanatic, and full of zealotry and arrogance if they wish their churches to grow. Such a suggestion shows more social scientific finesse than theological faithfulness. Some would empower people as much by the love of competition as by the love of people or of Christ. Cultural evolutionists have long contended that a cultural system which makes more efficient uses of the energy resources in a given environment will tend to prevail in it at the expense of those who less effectively exploit them. People with rifles to kill buffalo and Indians outlasted the Native Americans in most of the landscape. Thus the evolutionary instinct, the "selfish gene" of institutions, leads some to calculate: in our period, do people want intense experience and rigid authority? Then we must reformulate Christianity to meet their needs, which become the energy resources of the environment. And in meeting these needs, we will prevail at the expense of others. We must study people's deprivations, their hungers, their desires. Instead of asking which of these Christian faith may legitimately appeal to, we must calculate how to lure them, and then to pounce.

Similarly, Adam Smith's name came and went too fast. Just as Darwin is only a symbolic name for cultural evolution and the strategies based on it, so Smith dare not receive all the credit or blame for his contributions to modernity and evangelization. But political scientist David Apter quite properly seized on Smith's *The Wealth of Nations* as a symbol to recognize that, at a certain point in the West and the world, people no longer felt fated in the economic order. Once upon a time a believer was destined to nobility and wealth. The message of religion was to give alms, not to worship wealth, to steward it well, to be aware of its temptations. To be born poor destined one to life in the ranks of the poor. The message to the poor was not to rise into the middle class but to be content with poverty, to be submissive in servitude and pious until the afterlife, when accounts would be evened for the righteous.

Then through a centuries-long process that came to fulfillment late in the eighteenth century, people broke the sense of fate. Now they began to make rational calculation and choice: Do I invest in rum or slaves, in this ship or that ship or no ship? Both risks and yields increased. The entrepreneur broke the bounds of destiny and took on his own fate. Capitalism entered a new stage. The economic competitive model, focused on rational calculation and choice, became the paradigm of all modernity.

Including, we may add, modernity in religion. When the fiery spiritual awakener rode into a New England town in the 1740s, people who previously were fated to be under the ministry of a settled pastor in the only local church now were forced to choose. Do you want to be ministered to by an unsaved pastor, which meant one who could not date a conversion experience? Or do you and a converted minister wish to be assured of salvation? What do you do, then, when a second evangelist rides into town and asks the same question of people in both established and already awakened churches? Who is *really* saved and safe? Soon there would be in each town not only First and Second Congregational Churches but also First and Second Baptist Churches, and, almost 250 years later, Hare Krishna and Jews for Jesus and all. As is the case in the Smithian model, the shopper calculates carefully which choice is likely to be most productive.

This approach to church life also colors the strategy of Christians. Dare a local church that wants to convert people take a stand on ethical issues, like housing or nursing care? Dare a church body in the midst of an evangelism drive engage in anything of a controversial character and risk becoming unattractive, or burdened by secondary concerns and thus distracted from evangelizing? The advice is clear: Tailor the product. Organize all resources toward church growth. Compromise conscience. Appeal to prejudice. Muffle witness. The individual enterpriser in evangelism has an advantage over more diffuse congregations and church bodies which have to keep several other interests in mind. The rigorous evangelist has to appeal only to contemporary hungers for experience, identity, and authority.

After this little accounting, the basic question haunts: Is this what evangelizing is all about? Is Christ a presence in the world to satisfy the "junglelike" interests of the selfish gene or the jugular interests of competitive economics? What does all this striving do to people's rights, integrity, or outlook on the world? In the words of the late Jimmy Durante, "Why doesn't everybody leave everybody else the hell alone?"

A good question. A nation of metaphysical shoplifters and ideological window-shoppers finds many searchers picking, choosing, and grabbing until they have little core personality left. Many of the boasted statistics of conversions make little sense. If all those converts claimed by competitive evangelists joined the churches and stayed there, more than 100 percent of the population would be church members by now. Millions are cycling through the revolving door of reconversions, or playing musical chairs as they go from one movement of evangelism to another. As a result it is hard to picture some dabblers doing much but seeking thrills as they define their taste for sensation until they become jaded. Fanaticism results, as they redouble their efforts, having lost their goals. Their gospel is packaged, trivialized.

All true. But let it also be noted that not one thing in the last seven paragraphs has had anything to do directly with Christian evangelism. It all has to do with Darwin and the landscape, Smith and the free market, but never anything derived from the person, work, or words of Jesus. Christian evangelism does go on in the world we have just described, but it seeks a different definition. So the public church finds itself with a task that needs heroic reconceptualizing. Here the "civil" mainline and Catholic participants need the "committed" evangelicals, and vice versa to express more of the fullness of the whole church.

Scholars in the field work to establish precise definitions of evangelism. Conferences, libraries, and books devote themselves to dispute over this word which, like other basic terms, remains elusive. But we can stake out a space for a definition. This one must be unsatisfying, both to those predators who are sure evangelism means pounce, and to those half-committed antievangelists who are also sure it means pounce. To evangelize is to meet people in situations where the Gospel of Jesus Christ is given the opportunity to change them, as individuals and groups, and to bring them toward wholeness—in other words, to "save" them and to situate them in the context of Christian community, so that their lives will be enhanced and so that they can face together those questions of values, meanings, and service that also have eternal dimensions. Evangelizers are the agents of this task, and all participants are evangelizers, though some may have special callings to intensify the task. From historical surveys of them, it is possible to draw some conclusions about evangelizers. Prime among these is the understanding that they employed a clarified Christian focus. That is, they knew they had a specific story to tell, a community of faith to represent, a definite process to encourage. They did not use the term "evangelize" for generalized doing good or inspirational talk.

Evangelizers' activities were further marked by intentionality. They knew what they were doing. Many attracted converts simply by the example of their way of life. However creditable this magnetism was, it did not go under the name of evangelizing. Instead of waiting for occasional conversions, they calculated various means for carrying out their purposes and developed ways of measuring success or justifying failures.

All those who accomplished evangelism until very recently relied on the language of a community. Evangelizing does more than merely recognize "anonymous Christianity," to use Karl Rahner's language. Christians can often discern a Christic way among people who do not know the name of Jesus, but they prefer other terms for what they discover in them. Talk about a "Christian presence" has something to do with evangelism, but as Pierre Teilhard de Chardin said, "A presence is never mute." Sooner or later, a language rooted in scripture and tradition but embodied in a living and beckoning community erupts.

While the newest mass and electronic evangelists seem to work in isolation and while they often denigrate or bypass local churches, they live off support from them. If they cannot find communions in which to place their converts, they create clienteles or coteries for themselves. No matter how individualistic, they make their appeal by reference to other converts who have already accepted the Christian message and tie.

Next, evangelizers always imply personal involvement between themselves and the evangelized. They try to customize their appeals. A person with a goiter and a broken marriage can write in for counsel to a television evangelizer. An automated typewriter taped to a computer will then produce a letter of response assuring "Dear Mrs. Thornkild" that the evangelist will personally pray for her. She, receiving goiter letter #26 linked with troubled marriage letter #52, will feel intimately addressed.

Many aggressive evangelizers are ambivalent about the holistic approach. The belligerents do not like it because they find it a distraction from verbal evangelizing. Moderates believe it is confusing because they know other legitimate words to use for other legitimate activities. But both of these have been forced on the basis of biblical argument to see their work in the larger context and many have tailored their efforts accordingly.

No longer does a vivid sense of the whole Christian community vivify Christian evangelism, if it ever did. Evangelism has become a specialty of specialists. Part of the church carries the message to new people as part of its task. The whole nation and the whole church have little concern with it.

No longer are people easily brought to a protective turf, where all the symbols support the faith. Intense evangelizers therefore have to make more strenuous efforts than before to guard recruits. While a specific version of faith will set a cultural tone in some parts of the country—Baptist in the South, Mormon in the Great Basin, Lutheran in the upper Midwest, and the like—mass media, public education, and other influences invade all communities. For mainline Christians this intrusion has often meant such open exposure that the loyalties of their members become weak. Constrictive personality types have to compensate for their temptations to be lured elsewhere by becoming extremely rigid.

No longer are converts situated for life in the community that first attracted them. In the Darwinian-Smithian pattern, they are fair game for still other converters. Restlessness remains among those who find that someone is constantly bidding for their attention. Custodians of each community know that people can escape it.

No longer does biblical religion have a monopoly among the voices of evangelizers. Once there were only subtle variations between creeds of Protestant Christians. Now the voice of the evangelizer is lost among or takes on the color of the secular advertiser or the advocate of occult or other esoteric faiths. This pluralizing alters the character of loyalty by converts to the Christian word.

No longer does a religious assumption dominate the whole larger community. A far higher percentage of Americans belongs to churches now than in earlier centuries, and a larger number claims conversion. But the unconverted of long ago existed in a culture that secreted Christian laws, mores, and signals. Now even the converted live in a pluralistic and in many ways secular culture. Therefore, the militant converters fear leakage by their loyalists back into the larger culture. The constrictive types have to work harder than ever to spin a cocoon around the converts. They create Christian Yellow Pages, television networks, publishing empires, and cells.

No longer do the evangelized practically picture their commitment as being lifelong. Their pledges are firm, but evidence from sequential conversions suggests that they have only accepted the best deal "for now." The recruits have found their personal salvation to last for eternity—until the next bidder comes along.

These "no longers" serve as cold water baths to those who bring old assumptions about nurture from Catholicism and mainline Protestantism to their task. After the baths much reappraisal of evangelizing is going on. The temptation is strong for all but zealots to drop out of evangelizing, lest they be seen as players in a pathetic cultural game. An opposite temptation leads mainline Christians to try to import the techniques of the high powered and then to graft them onto the general outlook of those who are neither belligerent nor fanatic. Both responses divert from the wholistic Christian task.

In the public church, or for those who wish to see evangelism as a gift among several in the church, there is no point in their trying to outdo the competitors. Instead, these participants are learning to be faithful to the entire task of the church. They have to resist the temptation to measure the integrity of their life by whether or not they are growing or declining. One can grow or decline for the wrong reasons. The special gift of the public church is to relate the evangelistic impulse to the ecumenical outlook. How does one evangelize in an ecumenical context?

First, the public church speaks a word of judgment against those who too readily pit the dimensions of church life against each other. "Your God is too small," must be the word to those who work with the God of the tribe. This predator deity allows followers no choice but to see all people as having value only as prospective converts. The churches of these followers regard the "unsaved" as being unable to contribute to the ordering of life. The God who is the Lord of history, all history, however, is witnessed to as being active beyond the circles of those who will come to explicit faith. To say this is not to lapse into cheap universalism. (All universalisms somehow get to be dubbed cheap.) Instead, those who tell the Christian story and try to embody its motifs know that, at the end of the day, after they have tried to be faithful, they have to turn things back to God. They are "unprofitable servants." They have done all they could within the plan of God as revealed to them. How God acts beyond the context of that plan to people of other faiths or of no explicit faith remains in the realm of mystery.

The cynic in the wings, on whom we have called several times, can here charge forth and say that it is much easier and more effective to "preach hellfire and damnation." But that cynic has not read the polls. While during recent revivals more Americans were added to the number of those who believe in the devil than in God, they have not accompanied this belief with fear of such a devil. Already in 1952, fewer than one-eighth of those in the minority who believed there was a hell felt that it was any kind of threat to them. The negative images which frighten people today are aloneness, lack of identity, failure to be part of a group, addiction to drugs, and the like. One who listens carefully to conservative and militant evangelists alike will hear all but a few of them making positive appeals. They stress the advantages of life in their circle.

Evangelism in the public church means moving beyond the Enlightenment game of comparing deities and coming to intellectual judgments as to their relative worths. In a society with millions of uncommitted people who signal that they are on a search, there is no reason for competitive Christians to set up shops and argue their superiorities. The modest and honest have to admit that there are not only flaws in their Christian communities but also gaps in the Christian scheme. This is a faith built of "broken symbols," and not of immediate and potent answers for everything. The cross of Jesus Christ stands over against human efforts to find neat answers to the eternal puzzles. Christian evangelizers do not prove the existence of God or come up with logically satisfying answers to the problem of evil. They invite people to live in the context of death and rising, of cross and glory—but never to a stopping place, a journey's end on earth.

Evangelizing then becomes a matter of inviting people to the search for Christian meaning and belonging. In the public church evangelicals will pursue their direct form of witness, but will also make room for those whose way of evangelizing differs somewhat. The goal is not always and only to get another person to say, "I have found my personal redeemer." That is a legitimate form of ministry, but the Catholic Christian is likely to seek ways to incorporate others into the believing communion where the personal attachment matures.

In the interactive and ecumenical church, the whole community becomes the inviting agency. Of course, individuals must put themselves on the line for the community to be credible. Surveys show that four out of five people who become part of active Christian churches come to them through the word and example of people who were already important to them: spouses, relatives, friends, teachers, and the like. But these invite prospects not to a sect, a cult, a club, or least of all not to consumerism, so that the convert picks and chooses elements of faith over which he or she takes control. The inviters bid others instead to a living if flawed community. They welcome people to share in its quest, to examine its scope.

The beckoning relates to another meaning of the word "inviting." This living but flawed community must be inviting in the sense of attractive. To serious people this need not mean that the participants be glad-handers, compulsive smilers, or public relations geniuses. The church will make demands and make no secret of the fact that newcomers will share its struggles. But if the Christian circle looks closed, the presence of God is dim, and the program is complete without the role of the new participants. They will move on, and with good reason.

The public church as a whole will have access to cohorts of the population that have rejected existing patterns of evangelizing. In the interstices between these are all sorts of people who do not find them attractive. These citizens also signal that they need meaning. Analyst J. Russell Hale indicated how varied this half of the public, called the "unchurched," is. Hale provided an elaborate if informal set of labels. Some are mere dropouts. They include anti-institutionalists who feel "boxed in" by institutions which thwarted them. Others feel used, burned out by churches that are unresponsive to other interests of their life. There are apathetic types, drifters, cop-outs, "happy Hedonists," and the "locked out." This final class includes the rejected, the discriminated against.

Some are unchurched because they live in the anonymity of high-rise apartments, or are nomads beyond the range of settled communities. There are publicans who find the churches full of Pharisees and those they consider self-righteous belongers. Hale also located the scandalized who with good reason turned off the Christian community because of its moral faults. Last of all, he reminded, one can even spot a few "true unbelievers" who find no reason to affirm a divine call.

An alert public church, because of its internal varieties, is in a position to diagnose these passed-over and picked-over people who are not attractive to the noisier evangelists. The passed over are legion, and the pickings will not be slim. But somehow at present, the several churches in local communities tend to converge on the same few prospects, at the expense of the ecumenical commitment they have so expensively cultivated.

In the end, then, the ecumenical issue has less to do with remote committees in Rome, Geneva, or New York than with day-to-day competition and cooperation in the market of American communities. The local believers find that an annual joint Thanksgiving service is a wan expression of the unity they know they have. Today, leaders of local churches find their members at ease with those of other churches as seldom before. Most of them ignore what their theological committees discuss at a distance. They find it possible to unite on causes that call forth immediate Christian response: housing needs, migratory workers, Bible study, distribution of health services, prayer, care of the aged. They know that in their diversity each church may minister to a different segment of the community. But they bind themselves sufficiently to one another so that they all *do* mourn when one of them mourns and they all *do* rejoice when another of them rejoices. In such communities the act of inviting new members to one of the constituents is not a threat to others but an enhancement of the whole. When evangelism links with the whole work of the one church, diverse though it be, will the response be negative to the question: "Is Christ divided?"

6

Private Faith and Public Order

To various extents, citizens and participants in Christian communion all lead both public and private lives. So it is profitable to use what people, "we all," already know as a basis for moving toward more complicated attempts to relate public and private faith.

"We all" lead public lives by our very existence in modern civil societies. No one escapes taxes or licensing, and whether or not people engage in minimal acts of citizenship like voting, the society impinges on their lives in countless ways. And we all lead private lives. No one escapes death, which is the final lonely act. Even in a society whose media penetrate marital bedrooms or the chambers of monks, and in which instruments for surveillance are commonplace, people cherish zones of privacy.

We all nurture at least half-formed theories as to how these two spheres of life interact. Not many people take time to bring these to the front of the mind, to say nothing of articulating them. But without the help of Aristotle or Jesus, people carry in the back of their minds some vision of what belongs to public and private life. "A man's home is his castle." "That just isn't *done* in public." "Get out the vote." "Render to Caesar the things that are Caesar's and to God the things that are God's." "Separate church and state." "You can't have a look at my books." "Show me the search warrant." These and countless similar phrases grow from the thought people have given about when and how public and private life intersect or stay apart.

We all have forms of faith that we consider private but that have a public bearing. A member of the Supreme Court reported accurately when he observed that Americans "are a religious people." This was a social statement about their public condition. Yet most of the citizens would go on to say that the Court was commenting on their own private decisions. The poll-takers indicate that more than nine out of ten Americans believe in God, more than six out of ten belong to religious organizations, and that more than two out of three of these attend them with some regularity. But the polls are based on interviews with people who consider their choice to attend or not to attend a matter of personal and private decision. Not to participate *is* to take a stand on the role of faith in the life of "a religious people."

We all stand in traditions that help shape our decisions. In the lives of some people these traditions are both impressive and oppressive. Whether persons live in Tibet, Zaire, China, or Iran, makes a difference to their faith, in both public and private life. Closer to home, it may well make a difference whether the individual lives in the Hassidic Jewish neighborhoods of Williamsburg in Brooklyn, a small Southern and hence Baptist town, a Norwegian and therefore Lutheran valley in Minnesota, or an impersonal high-rise in mobile and consequently secular Manhattan. To some extent it remains true that our context tilts us in certain directions even in a plural society. José Ortega y Gasset once challenged: "Tell me the landscape in which you live and I will tell you who you are." The Methodist minister looking out the window of a Kansas church can do this better than the New Yorker looking down from a skyscraper, but the people around them in many ways are more predictable than they know in both settings.

As with place, so with time: to know that one lived in a Jewish ghetto or shtetl in the Pale of Europe in 1881, on the Kentucky frontier during the revivals of 1801–02, or in the evangelical capital of Wheaton, Illinois, in the 1980s is to receive some clue as to how a citizen is likely to relate personal decision or private life to public outlook and faith.

We all experience change in these traditions. Sometimes the change produces resistance, as it did when Iranian Shi'ite Muslims or American fundamentalists tried to keep modernity at a distance. Each Muslim or fundamentalist may feel that he or she is making a personal choice, yet so predictable is the pattern of choice that we sense how much it occurs within a tradition. An American who wants to go back to good old days has a different memory than does an Iranian. Each society tends to take a particular passage to modernity or in opposition to it, and each society will also tend to keep on appealing to the values it carried through that passage, whether those values are believed to be biblical, Marxist, "enlightened," or whatever.

We all take attitudes toward such change. Some move reluctantly, in the spirit of conservative Edmund Burke: "If it is not necessary to change, it is necessary not to change." Others recognize the wisdom of Richard Hooker: "All change is inconveniencing, including change from worse to better." And still more will embrace the spirit of John Henry Newman: "To grow is to change and to have grown much is to have changed often." In all three cases, problems result with change, especially among people who are uprooted and assaulted. They like to feel that they are masters of their fate and captains of their soul, and yet they have to cope with change induced by crises in public order.

Finally, and this is especially the case in our time, we all experience and create abrasions because of these problems. The temptation then grows for reactors to deny the nature of public existence, to turn uncivil. Such are not safe times, as public and private worlds collide.

One simple case study illustrates all these points. For a hundred years one wing of conservative American Protestantism conceived of itself and was largely concerned with private faith. It was shaped by revivalism, with its call for personal decision, and issued in an economic outlook that its advocates called individualistic. The leaders made no effort to encourage participants to express their faith in the public order. At least, they had no consistent policy on the basis of which to urge them. Most of them made an exception in the era of battles over Prohibition, when they linked up with public-minded liberal Protestants to make and then try to keep America dry. When their own group felt threatened, some of them spoke up, but then when the challenge passed, they receded.

After the middle of this century, this "private" party found a foil when public Protestantism, at least through its leaders, began to speak up on issues of civil rights, poverty, social justice, and the Vietnamese War. By this time some of the revivalists, even though they claimed they were in the world chiefly to rescue people out of it, did transgress their old lines. Historian Erling Jorstad has written of their efforts as being *The Politics of Doomsday*. Crusaders like evangelist Billy James Hargis engaged in what they called circuit-riding against liberals. A Church League of America claimed to be preventing America from falling to a church-led conspiracy for atheistic communism. But most of the "private" Protestants were content to watch these antagonists go at it, while they set out to save souls in evangelism campaigns and to provide warm cocoons of organizational life around their converts and colleagues.

Late in the 1970s when they attained sufficient power and experienced provocation, millions changed their outlook. They began to claim that there was no place to escape the public realm. Decisions made in Congress or the Supreme Court enhanced or violated their personal ways of living and thinking. Thus the prohibitions against Bible reading for devotion in schools or legal permission of abortions looked to them like intrusions on their own faith and conviction. They also began to learn that there were enough of them around to make an impact on local, state, and federal governments if only they found a voice with which to assert themselves. Finally, they found that voice through leaders who knew how to use modern media, especially television and direct mail.

Some of the militant leaders like television evangelist Jerry Falwell made no secret of the fact that they were switching ideologies from private to public commitment. Consistency did not disturb him in the face of what he saw to be urgent moral problems and his own opportunity to assert power. Falwell believed belligerently in an inerrant Bible, one that cannot be mistaken in any sort of detail—certainly not on an issue as crucial as the relation of private faith to public morals. Nor was there any doubt in his mind that he interpreted that inerrant Bible inerrantly. He wielded it before an audience and said, as he admitted he had done in 1968, that "the Bible says" that all clergy should stay out of politics and that the church should not take political stands. There was no doubt then that he heard himself speaking up for the unchanging will and word of God. Yet by 1980 as he entered wholeheartedly into the realm of legislation and the selection of political candidates, Falwell still appealed to that inerrant Bible which he again claimed to be interpreting inerrantly. The fundamentalist admitted that he had changed, but he made it seem as if his was a change of policy, not of doctrine.

Some leaders were more subtle. They disguised their change by claiming that they were even now not participating in public life or in the political order. Thus when they gathered 175,000 people in an effort to mobilize 1,000,000 for a "Washington for Jesus" rally in the spring of 1980, they beguiled many followers into believing that this was nothing but an expression of piety and morality, not of politics. Advance criticism led them to mute their political sounds, sounds widely advertised in their advance publicity. Yet the selection of Washington as a site, the rhetoric and cadence of their homilies, and their illustrations of what was wrong and what could be right about America involved them constantly in political reference. They made no secret of their desire to promote constitutional amendments against abortion and for school prayer, or to push for legislation against obscenity, the Equal Rights Amendment, or pornography. All these promotions involved budgets and ballots, lobbies and legislatures. Mass communicators and politicians certainly were aware of this rally and what it symbolizes as a political intrusion.

Liberal religious leaders, veterans of public encounter, were equally aware. Instead of seeing that the new militants were merely changing the rules in order to enter a familiar political game, or instead of contenting themselves with criticism of the content of the belligerents' messages, many of them issued press releases bemoaning the new efforts to "blur the line between church and state" or to "mingle religion and politics." The inner contradiction of such criticism coming from the leaders of public churches was apparent to the citizenry and thus was of little effect.

More valid was a set of questions concerning the newcomers' perceptions of what the public order was or should be. In many respects, their choice of issues reflected historic interests of private-minded conservative Christians, whether Catholic or Protestant. They had to do with legislation in areas where private vice or virtue collided: the bedroom, the clinic, the cycles of personal life. The militants devoted themselves less to questions of justice, equality, or addressing poverty and hunger—though many of them as individuals may well have been humane about such issues—and tried instead to impose their private vision on the public realm. Thus efforts to have America legally declared a Christian nation or attempts in the ethos to "call America back to Christ" in the name of the founding fathers who two centuries before had resisted such appeals, were denials of the character of American pluralism. If their way were followed to its logical conclusion, they would encompass the public order with a totalist Christianism.

Whatever their fate, whether their change represents a permanent power shift or a temporary foray in American public life, they do serve as a case study to illustrate all of the "we all's" in our sequence above. They lead both private and public lives. They work on the basis of theories as to how these relate. They act on the foundation of their faiths as these issue from traditions. They react because of change in their traditions when these seem under attack. They make the passage to public life inelegantly, a sign that it is full of problems. And their passage creates abrasions between them and others in the public order.

Whoever repeals the record of the very recent past will easily see that long histories lie behind both the traditional sides. On one hand are those who self-consciously recognize and long have recognized a commitment to relate private faith to public order through what we are calling a public church. On the other hand are or were those who, just as self-consciously though perhaps with some delusions, believed they could box in or compartmentalize each of these two spheres of their existence. This is not the place for a full dress rehearsal of the prehistories, but a quick turning of the pages illumines the reasons for tension today.

Following Robert Bellah's evolutionary stage-theory of religious history, one can see that the public party has the longer and larger history. In what Bellah calls primitive and archaic societies there was little splitting up, little differentiation between what later eras in the West called church and state. No consistent hierarchy of priests withstood ranks of royalty in a civil order. Of course, individuals led more or less private lives in their huts, caves, and hearts, but all the ordering of their existence was somehow collective, binding them to a specific way of looking at nature and spirit.

Following those two types of society there came the era of historic religious foundings such as those of Judaism, Christianity, Islam, Buddhism, and Hinduism within a couple of thousand years, which means within a second of geological time and a few minutes of human time. It is impossible to know or to agree upon what was in the minds of leaders like Moses, Jesus, Muhammad, and Buddha. But whatever their separate and separatist intentions, the cultures that surrounded the heritages of their faiths and outlooks wrapped private faith in public trappings. Ancient Israel was an open theocracy in which God, not the people, *theos* not *demos,* ruled. After Jesus and Muhammad there came Christendom and Islamdom, to use Marshall Hodgson's apt term for the latter development. Even today one cannot extricate Eastern religion from its public cultures, and the presence of modernity against its own background differs from Western developments also because of the spiritual outlook in the surrounding public order.

A fourth era called early modern, very brief though it was, indicated strains within historic public orders. Thus in the Western Reformation: in the main its leaders did not separate "church and state" or, in a different category, private and public faith and life, but they did introduce pluralism into Christendom. Eventually heirs of reform had to come to terms with the emerging order. Two centuries later, with the rise of the Enlightenment and its new religious presuppositions, many in the Western world set out to chop apart church and state, private faith and public order, religion and society.

In a fifth period, the modern—and which now verges on what some impulsively call postmodern—cultural resolutions complete what the early moderns began to do. The modern era finds its themes in the chopping up of life and the impelling of choice upon private citizens. For the Jew, these meant that one began to separate ethnicity from faith. An author at last could write an article on "Why I choose to be a Jew." Once upon a time, and even on the books today, to be born of a Jewish mother made one a Jew. Now, however, a Jew could choose to pass as a Gentile, could convert to Christianity and become a "Jew for Jesus," or could become part of that large cohort of Jews who turned out to be fair game for Eastern and occult faiths.

For European Catholicism, the trauma occurred formally as "the separation of church and state." In America, the suffering establishment was non-Roman Catholic, Congregational in the North and Episcopal in the South. But throughout the West it was Catholicism that set the pattern and had most to lose through anticlericalism and separationist revolutions. Everywhere there rose secular religions or religious nationalisms to counter the old unifying and public claims of what we might call Catholicdom. As many observers have pointed out, ever after this time, being a Catholic became a matter of choice, a datum of private existence that only accidentally might bear on public order. "I happen to be a Catholic" is a frequent though once upon a time unheard of, inconceivable expression.

Late coming, and especially American, Protestants to some extent shared both these traumas. Where their cultures broke down and they entered pluralism, their young also found it easy to drift into private but untraditional faiths. Many of them dropped out into secular culture, mild agnosticism, or Eastern and occult faiths. Being Scotch-Irish no longer meant being Presbyterian, being Swiss no longer meant being Reformed, and being Swedish no longer predisposed one to being Lutheran. Similarly, separation of church and state meant abrasions not only for European established Protestants or colonial American Congregationalists and Episcopalians as these lost their establishments. It also meant that Protestants had to establish themselves in the mores and the ethos in efforts to develop Protestantdom without benefit of law. In the past century they have had to yield turf within it as the number of non-Protestantants grew within their cultures.

In some respects, Protestantism compensated for legal losses by winning territories and trying to hold on to them. Through the revivals they captured much of the American South. Through nineteenth-century continental immigration up the Mississippi or along the new rail routes, they created a regional culture around the Great Lakes, along the Great Rivers, on the Great Plains, and thanks to the Mormon egress, in the Great Basin.

Later, through expansion of their middling economic classes, for some time they held the suburbs as their fiefdoms. But after World

6 2 0 2 4

War II a new pluralism led the urban South to attract non-Protestants. Urbanization changed the "Great" countries and the suburbs lured Jews, Catholics, and others who did not fit in. So for Protestants a trauma or turmoil comparable to Catholic separation of church and state or Jewish division of religion from ethnicity also had to do with a chopping up, a separation between region and reflexive religion. Protestant faith and life became easily escapable and survived chiefly as a datum of personal existence.

One could even add that a fourth American faith experienced a tumult almost from the beginning because it was born at a time when the turmoil had already begun. This was the faith of the Enlightenment, the mild but focused Deism of founding fathers like George Washington, Benjamin Franklin, Thomas Jefferson, and James Madison. All of the founders except for Charles Carroll of Carrollton were of Protestant stock. Most of them remained church members. All of them believed that public order and public virtue had something to do with each other and that public virtue was grounded in a religious sensibility or commitment. Most of them helped "separate church and state" and produce an order which a later Supreme Court described as "wholesomely neutral" about religion. They were not "wholesomely wholesome" in an open advocacy of a particular established faith. Nor were they "neutrally neutral" to the extent that they really left religion alone simply by excluding loyalty to its forms from their national Constitution. They gave as a heritage the uneasy combination of adverb and adjective: "wholesome neutrality" could never produce a sense of permanent resolution or quiet.

Most of these founders, as remarked earlier—Benjamin Franklin most notably—did dream of a new order of public religion, one which made room for what they called "the sects." Those who felt most benign toward the sects expected them to form a kind of community of communities. Each could pursue its own vital creeds and values, however irrelevant each seemed to members of others. Meanwhile, they would dip into a common treasure of commitments to the public weal that they dispensed in their peculiar ways. Those like Jefferson who were most suspicious about these so-called sects were more overt about their dream of replacing their peculiarities with a new common faith of natural reason, natural law, and natural rights. Such founders succeeded in establishing their common faith as a basis for many national institutions, and to this day this faith suffuses many public expressions of faith.

Their dream, however, was deferred and an early schism in the culture denied their implied monopoly. Within a generation after the national founding, Protestant America underwent particular revivals that issued in competitive churches. Almost all of the church-goers challenged the Deist content of the founders' faith. The rest pretended it away by converting these founders posthumously to orthodox Christianity. Even fundamentalists who would today reject Washington, Franklin, and Jefferson from their churches as danger-ous Unitarians, tend to endorse them after two centuries and claim that as Christians these were founding a privileged Christian repub-lic.

A faith, however, that to enlightened statesmen looked inclusive and common appeared very exclusive and particular to its oppo-nents. The revivalists in the name of piety set out to stamp out its temple of reason. They largely succeeded, at least in the churchly culture, though less so among intellectual and literary figures. Where they did not prevail, the temple still fell into decay. Today it would be hard to find a university philosophy department that teaches En-lightenment thought as the truth about life. The original public creed joins its counterparts as a competing sect, and at its best it interacts symbiotically with the other elements in the national community of communities.

The new empire combined the heirs of Protestant revivalism, the newly activated Catholic and Jewish immigrants, and believers in some homegrown faiths. Each of these put their major energies into providing enclosed, almost larval existence for their participants. Competition led to prosperity and confusion. In times when people felt under pressure to choose to have faith or to choose among faiths, those emphases that accented private benefit over public obligation have prospered. That is why in modern and now postmodern reli-gion the private heresy overtook the public tradition. And that may be why antimoderns, bewildered and stunned by choice, want to repeal modernity and go back to easier, earlier America. By name and by law they would make this a more homogeneous Christian nation, and produce third-class citizens out of "secular humanists" and devotees of pluralism and choice.

While the creators of congregations have been capable of creating successful subcommunities, they often did so while giving lip ser-vice to the ideology of rugged individualism in religion. This ten-dency was eventually to work against them as citizens carried their new logic of spiritual privation to its extreme. Some left or lost the old faiths, some found new ones. In either case they showed that they had become moderns through their developed sense that faith was nothing but a private affair. In this respect, they borrowed ideol-ogy or outlook from people outside the Christian camp. Thomas Jef-ferson had said he would not go to heaven if he must go with a group, a sect. Thomas Paine, his contemporary, averred that his own mind was his church. More than a century later, William James defined religion as momentous private choice and Alfred North Whitehead as what one did with solitariness. Little wonder that in the face of such attractions, public faith in its social forms, the public church and the civil public religion, came to be unsatisfying to so many.

From these brief descriptions of constantly changing party lines it is easy to see why abrasions result. Prophets of change are aware of these, and relish them. James Robison, a militant fundamentalist who tried to produce a Christian America over against secular humanist and liberal religious America, delighted in the conflict: "Tell me one prophet who didn't divide." Not many would disagree with the fact that prophets usually do divide, and the religiously informed would agree that sometimes prophets validly must divide. But this understanding did not lead the public to abdicate responsibility from the task of testing the prophets, to see whether the causes citizens chose merited support or would issue in valid forms of dividing. When opponents of fundamentalism spoke up, new conflict resulted. A consequence was the clash between styles: civil discourse appropriate to the public order versus barbarian expressions that would issue in the end of discourse.

To introduce the term "civil" at this stage is to deal in an ambiguity or at least in a kind of pun. Civil religion, to follow Robert Bellah's use of Jean-Jacques Rousseau's concept, is an overarching, undergirding, institutionalized ideology, a broadly limned faith for a whole national society. This civil religion exists both within and alongside the church. More recently, however, debate has moved from the national forms of civil religion to those that we might properly describe as a pattern of manners, a modality of behaviors, in a society whose members do not agree about the role of religion and the rights of religionists.

Historian and social analyst John Murray Cuddihy has done as much as anyone to inquire about and then to criticize the theory and practice of being civil in religious manners. His analysis of modernity as a chopping up of existence and an impelling of choice matches, indeed informs, the analysis just given here. Cuddihy sees that as a result of its impulse, people confront a number of choices. They may set out to revoke modernity and then by coercion develop a "demodernized" total faith for a society—as Mao Zedong set out to do during China's revolution. But short of that, in free and pluralist societies, people compensate by becoming civil toward others, as private citizens or as members of other tribes. As Cuddihy sees it, not without traces of some ironies he half enjoys and paradoxes he does not resolve, they tend to turn civil at the expense of deep personal commitment. One of my dictionaries saw the term civility itself "sinking into 'decent politeness'," which may be one of the more bleak precincts of purgatory for any saving and vital faith.

Cuddihy and those who share his views say that it is all well and good for scholars and analysts to observe the onslaughts of modernity and what they do to once-secluded tribes and traditions. Scholars spend their years acquiring tools to cope with change, which they observe as if from the eye of a hurricane. Most people in their cultural shelters do not have that luxury. The hurricanes, unblunted, hit their shores and sweep away or blow over the little huts in which they have cherished private and traditional sets of meanings. A concrete example: most of the people of Iran were mere victims of technological, industrial, and social changes. Only the former Shah and selected elites received the mixed benefits of such transformations. In much of the West people will put up with many of the banes of modern change because they also share in the benefits. Not so in Iran. People believed in Sh'ite Islam and found it available to use as a tool for demodernizing. This meant that people could use it to regress to simpler, more intact social conditions. At least for a stage, they permitted their imams and priests to develop a clergy-run state. Back came the *chador* and the veil over women, sure signs of regress, thought liberated Westerners. They curtailed television with its jumble of signals, cinema and popular music with their jungle of sights and sound, and freedom of choice in religion for Baha'is, Sùnni Muslims, Jews, and stray Christians. Iranians could restore or thought they could restore their huts as these had been before the storms.

In the United States something of the same spirit was present in the reactive circles of those who took their private faith grievances into the public realm. Here modernization had proceeded too far to be rolled back. The intransigents had to select areas in which to engage in partial counterattack. Rather than shatter their television screens, they chose to live with them and to seize them as instruments of a cause. Unable either to overcome pluralism or control it, they created a network of stations and preempted a portion of the channels and hours for themselves. Unable to destroy the commercial book publishing industry, they established their own publishers and Ma and Pa bookstores through which to promote countervalues. Rather than continue to try to silence rock music, they set Jesus words to it while attacking the beat of rock performers who did not. Rather than acquiesce to a society whose pluralism annoyed and grieved them, they set out on forays to overcome selective offenses in it through legislation. They insisted on the teaching of the biblical doctrine of creation alongside the theory of evolution in the schools and wanted to impose times of meditation and prayer in public classrooms. They set out to promote constitutional amendments forbidding abortion or to prevent the passage of those that might change the traditional concept of how the sexes should relate. Theirs was a barbarian intrusion in the eyes of their enemies who had invented the game of churchly intervention in public life. To scholars in the eye of the hurricane they were merely being uncivil.

Calling them barbarians or uncivil people does nothing to uncongeal them or divert them from their crusades. Once fanaticism set in not all of them would be diverted, no matter what. Some of them acted demagogically, once they learned how to exploit discontent to gain power for themselves. Just as many more acted without awareness of consequences. In their huts they had experienced the sudden winds. They had not previously seized occasions to reflect on their own previous profitable investments in pluralism and civility. They would not lose their zeal because analysts or more civil opponents derided them. Such derision would only seem to them like the voice of Satan, who naturally would conspire with humanists to destroy the Lord's flocks. Creative efforts to address their world begin with the act of giving a hearing to their hurts and resentments. Efforts to reason them back into the inclusive public order follow.

To give some of them a hearing of sorts, let me reconstruct aspects of an interview I had some years ago with a Baptist during a Kanawha County, West Virginia, protest. Some aggrieved fundamentalists rejected the current high school textbooks. They connected their dissent to labor strikes by miners. Eventually violence led to the death of a couple of people. My reconstruction of the phoned conversation will put some words into the mouth of my conversation partner, though it will not put ideas into his head. The talk went something like this: "They give our kids science texts that contradict the beginnings of Genesis in our Bibles. They force sex education on them but God wants parents to instruct them. Their literature books include dirty words and sexy scenes. When they talk about morality, they allow the children choice where God does not. Should they tell white lies? Should they live with someone without being married? Now we think such books are dangerous. We know they go against all that we believe. At the very least, we want the bad stuff cut out of those books we have to use. More than that, we want to be represented in the texts that everyone uses. That is what we are fighting about.

"Look at it this way," my resentful interviewee went on.

"Everyone else has a liberation movement. It gives them power to change the books and the schools. Everyone else except us, that is, and we were here first. Because of women's lib all the texts got changed to 'he/she' where they used to say 'he,' and they can never show a woman in a bad light. The black movement saw to it that 'Sambo' disappeared because the white oppressor had put that there, just as the male oppressor once kept women down. So the Indians got into the act. Goodbye to cowboys-and-Indian stories. All Indians dead or alive were good Indians. The Jews see to it that Shakespeare goes, because of Shylock. You can't say anything critical of Catholics. Homosexual liberation reaches down into Junior High texts and changes everything in the face of normal, heterosexual 'oppressors.' We've watched the stories of all these liberations and exoduses. The one thing they all have in common in their story of their Moseses and exoduses is that *I have to be everybody else's Pharoah*. And we aren't going to take that anymore."

For civil citizens to compensate by giving equal time to white Appalachia or fundamentalist Protestantism no longer suffices. Resentment has turned to rage and that, mixed with a sense of power, leads the partisans to rework and rewrite the tradition and try to impose it on everyone else.

Just as a person must listen to their resentments and rages, so it becomes important to reason about the effects of their programs. The complainers were in a circumstance that George Bernard Shaw described as the one tragedy in life: not getting what they wanted. Now they would face his other tragedy in life: getting what they want. For example, many have not thought through what a school prayer amendment would mean. Many of them live in school districts where the vast majority of the children are fundamentalist Baptists or at least Baptists or Protestants or Christians—or are not offended culturally by any of these. For them an amendment would mean simply "going back" to the good old days before the Court decisions of 1962 and 1963. The contagion of this outlook has spread even to pluralist states like California, where there are strong movements to "put God back into the schools" after "the Supreme Court took God out" when it eliminated prayer and devotion in classrooms. They are unaware that the people themselves had long before done the eliminating, if that is what the absence of school prayer means. Richard Dierenfeld has shown that a bare 2 percent of California classrooms did have school prayer or devotion just before the Court decisions.

Had advocates of such an amendment envisioned the future in which it would restore school devotions? They give no evidence that they have reckoned with the problems of pluralism. By no means all fundamentalists or conservatives themselves share the desire on these terms to "put God back into the schools." Many of them hold to radical views of the separation of church and state. They see school prayer as a violation of these views. Others believe that all spiritual nurture belongs in the home and church. Even if they get past the obstacles posed by their fellow believers on the right, more are ahead. Let there be mere meditation? Not all religious groups advocate such uses of silence—witness the opposition by fundamentalists themselves to Transcendental Meditation as a false religion. During an earlier round of testimony before the House Judiciary Committee one congressman said that he saw nothing wrong with completely neutral gestures like asking the children to bow their heads, close their eyes, and fold their hands in order to make spiritual thoughts possible. Completely neutral? Up jumped a rabbi to remind him that the congressman had just described a very Christian posture which the rabbi as a Jew no more wanted imposed on his children than a Buddhist would.

If there are words of prayer, to whom are they addressed, and by whom? Would small children not soon show the same churlishness and the same rebellion "against God" that colleges experienced when chapel was compulsory? Who would see to it that child-led devotions were not bizarre or that teacher-led prayers were not amateurish and unthinking? How would teachers and parents protect the rights of objectors or guard them from being discriminated against? Conversely, how would they prevent majorities who received excuses not to participate on conscientious ground from being prejudiced against by the overtly pious? If children are to read spiritual texts devotionally who picks them? Majorities? If so, non-Mormons transferred to Utah will have to wait for a week or two to have a turn at the Bible in place of the Book of Mormon. Jehovah's Witness children would not hear their own translation of the Bible. They would have to bear with translations they are taught to think of as perverse. Christians would not hear and may not read the New Testament in the many schools where there is a Jewish majority. Will Mary Baker Eddy's *Science and Health with Key to the Scriptures* be a regular scripture where non-Christian Scientists find it offensive? Debates over such issues would be excellent learning experiences in public schools, but they are certainly not what the militant prayer amendment people have in mind. Those who have reduced the issue to power plays or bumper-sticker wars for their own political gain will not be convinced by efforts to point to problems. But these may well cause doubts among some of their followers. They cannot, after warnings, complain about the Brave New World when it arrives, thanks to their efforts.

My choice of these examples should not suggest that all barbarianism and incivility comes from such camps. America has seen just as potent and unthinking advocacies from the left and in the secular camps. This recent development merits notice because to many it appears to be a new phenomenon and because it stands the best chance of learning some tactics that will help make it prevail.

The new militants are making up one more tribe, much like the clan of the barbarian young back in the counterculture. Historian Theodore Roszak called their unkempt appearance, their assault on "Dad's World," and their protests against repressive tolerance, part of an "invasion of Centaurs" in the overordered temple of the civil Apollo. Most of the noisier advocacies across generational, sexual, age-cohort, ethnic, racial, and religious lines begin with an uncivil invasion. The agitators' terms, appearance, and demands are most militant at the earliest stages, as they make their presence known and felt. After that they can begin to compromise. It may be that uncivil religionists in America will soon reach that stage. They have some rights to both stages, the same rights as do their counterparts and competitors. They are not unique, only distinctively powerful.

Suppose they migrate to stage two. What will result, once they have ended the invasion and joined or rejoined the public order? To some the dream would be a society of agreement and perfect order, the *unum* of organic wholeness for which Plato yearned. Short of pure coercion—which did not even work in Maoist China—it is hard to picture that being the result, even if it were desirable. American society does not even have enough consensus about the consensus to get such a society going. A British observer, Bernard Crick, is wary of claims that all societies, including North America, ever need or have one. What, he asks, is the *consensus juris* behind law in Canada, "or anywhere, between Catholic, Protestant (High or Low), Muslim, Hindu, Jew, Sceptic, Agnostic, Freethinker, Atheist, and Erastian" people who share common political allegiances but few philosophical fundamentals? In America Crick found no other consensus than Groucho Marx's *cri de coeur:* "Take care of me. I am the only one I've got." Crick believes that societies like the American have no systematic or metaphysical consensus or cement beyond the activity of politics itself.

At the opposite extreme are those who advocate a consensus imposed by autocracy and based on religious values. Between them is the zone in which people as diverse as publicist Walter Lippmann and Jesuit John Courtney Murray staked out a "public philosophy."

This philosophy came down to some rudimentary version of natural law, the notion that in the structure of the universe or the given world there are the bases for political values and society. In American history the outlook finds prefigurement and embodiment in the Declaration of Independence, the tradition of republican and democratic thought, the legal heritage, and the Constitution.

Modern cultural and comparative anthropology have jostled the advocates of particular public philosophies. Somewhere or other one can find a set of tribes that legitimate murder, have no interest in recourse to law, no taboo against incest, nor any impulse toward regard for others. But the public philosophers, chastened but not silenced, at least work to discern enough *consensus juris* to create a zone in which the debate can occur. In John Courtney Murray's vision, one does not seek stifling agreement but challenging disagreement. Disagreement, which means understanding each other's thought world and terms and the reasons they hold, is hard to come by. People often confuse it with confusion. Confusion, which is what we normally think is disagreement, is easy to come by. The public order asks for nothing more to get started than for thoughtful, reasoning beings to be civil enough to get locked in argument toward public goods.

Murray, to his credit, did not believe that all incivility came from the McCarthyite right that was strong when the Jesuit wrote, nor from spittle-bearded and flaming fundamentalists with their atavistic impulses. He did not think that all his fellow Catholics were civil. Some of us saw him fume in the face of incivility in the Vatican itself. But he also did not think that the reasonable people of the Enlightenment who talked a civil style always embodied it. And he knew that liberal Protestants, who then were often still prejudiced against Catholicism as a thing in their way, could be barbarians. The new barbarian, he wrote, did not come carrying a club or wearing a bearskin. He might be clad in Brooks Brothers garb; she might wield a ballpoint pen and wear academic robes.

Civil society is political society, a world of conflicting interests between tribes. People found it on discourse that is often and at its best quite passionate. Such a society sets out to minimize the violence that naturally lurks in the human jungle and tries to protect and assure the interests of the groups in society. In that public order the separate believing communities have their place. Many of them may wish to overcome pluralism within history, but, says Murray, they cannot do this without total coercion—if then. They may, like him, be monists who believe that the final secret of history is One, unum, God. But for reasons they cannot fully elaborate, they will not find that oneness manifest in history. Pluralism, said the Jesuit, may be finally against the will of God. But it is the human condition. Pluralism is written into the script of history and dealt with the cards of politics. It will not marvellously cease to trouble the human city— least of all the one that wants to call itself free and to assure freedoms.

What has happened to the Lippmannite or Murrayite advocacies of civility? A John Murray Cuddihy would argue that these are all sham on the part of entrenched forces who ask for others to be civil so they can hold their place. Or they may be the marks of the simply tolerant who have not the passion to hold convictions and thus to be willing to coerce faith, as *real* believers always have done. Again, they may be the luxury of the informed scholars who are deft enough to cover the traces to their own prejudices, or adept at finding tools for analysis so they can sit in the eye of the hurricane and outlast it— until they can interpret all the swept away and blown over huts.

Civility yields to uncivil bumper-sticker warfare, where non-sequiturs posing as premises turn out to be conclusions. "Abortion Is Murder." "A Woman's Body Is Her Own to Do with What She Wants." "Guns Don't Kill People. People Kill People." "America: Love It or Leave It." "Make Love, Not War." Above such stickers there is never an invitation to reason. From under and behind them comes a blast of carbon monoxide.

When discourse breaks down tribal people are tempted to use politics in order to end politics. Some interest groups will simply try to exclude or silence others. They move from the private realm not to the public but immediately to a totalist zone that lives beyond the range of politics and publics. Pluralism and choice would end. If citizens are to restore the public order and ground civility in something of value, they have to appeal to more than tolerance. For this resource one must go deeper than we have to this point in understanding the values of the tribe and the values of the polis, the city with its interacting and open tribes.

Part Three

Tensions
of the Church
in Public

7

Tribes Versus Tribalism

T he intense subcommunities of American life function like tribes in the model that contrasts the values of the tribe and the city. The public church brings together numbers of these tribes into a kind of political complex. To do so does not violate the concept of the church as church. It is necessary merely to suspend or bracket views of other dimensions of churchly life in order to note and clarify this one aspect of its form. We could call the constituent tribes "mediating structures," as Peter Berger and Richard Neuhaus do when referring to petite forms like family, neighborhood, and parish. Or they could be the "little platoons" of which British thinker Edmund Burke spoke as he described forces that stood between the autonomous but beleaguered private self and the overwhelming social Leviathan. Or the tribe can be a kin to Aristotle's "association" where it best fits into the political sequence. Aristotle's teacher Plato had looked for pure consensus and social unity as he called for civil centralization at the expense of tribes, freedom, and tradition. Aristotle wanted to observe and keep discrete the elements that made up a more diverse public order, so he opposed philosophical unity that demanded coercion.

Aristotle began a famous section of his *Politics* with a rejoinder to Socrates, through whom Plato spoke: "The error of Socrates must be attributed to the false notion of unity from which he starts. Unity there should be, both of the family and of the state, but *in some respects only.* For there is a point at which a state may attain such a degree of unity as to be no longer a state, or at which, without actually ceasing to exist, it will become an inferior state, *like harmony passing into unison, or rhythm which has been reduced to a single foot*" [Emphasis mine]. For Aristotle, however, "similars do not con-

113

stitute a state." The state must make room for kinship, friendship, and other forms of traditional and unmeltable bonds. The good state makes room for dissimilarities and disparities between its constituents or associating elements. Aristotle went on: "Is it not obvious, that a state may at length attain such a degree of unity as to be no longer a state?—since the nature of a state is to be a plurality, and intending to great unity, from being a state, it becomes a family, and from being a family an individual; for the family may be said to be more one than the state, and the individual than the family. So that we ought not to attain this greatest unity even if we could, for it would be the destruction of the state."

Aristotle's model found few advocates, Cicero being a partial exception, until the time of toleration in the seventeenth century and in the Enlightenment that followed. Never is this model secure for long. Today, in order to counter Leviathan or the overunified state, some tribes have had to dig in, but they became merely tribalistic. Before making any value judgments, however, as to how particular groups fit into Aristotle's view of these mediating associations, it is necessary to do justice to a sampling of contemporary tribes, to understand their impulses.

The term came back to American public consciousness because of the new articulateness of Native Americans. In the 1960s they began to speak up for the values of their tribes against the encroaching bureaucracy and the media of the white world. Never mind that the term tribe was itself a white person's imposition. Most Native Americans had simply conceived of their people as "The People." It happened that the tribal term became useful, and they adopted it. The word stuck, and from time to time it reappears in reassertions of Native American life. To the Indian it symbolizes an unmalleable world, a "package deal" of resistance through which Native Americans can find meaning and belonging. They relate as tribes to nature and their environment, to the spirits behind these, to practice and tradition, and, cognitively, to the myths that lay behind the origin of their people and all people. Through such rites and myths the heirs of the first Americans ward off chaos and the threat of enemies or bad circumstances.

Concurrently with the Native American self-consciousness came the revival of African tribal life, long before transported for centuries to America but never forgotten. The word "the Roots phenomenon" entered the vocabulary, thanks to a popular television series. Whatever its flaws, the series succeeded in showing blacks and nonblacks alike that their origins were not in Harlem or in sharecropping on plantations. They had not lost all Africanity during Atlantic mid-passage or the seasoning in the American slave compounds. They were not a blurry mass of lookalike blacks. They had separate histories, identities, locales, and memories in diverse African tribes and stories.

Most religious Americans grew up thinking of tribes as issuing from Israel and its twelve tribes. The Hebrew Scriptures were the primal stories for Jews, and many a child could map the locales of Reuben, Simeon, Dan, and all the rest, and knew what Levi represented. Modern Jewish self-consciousness after the Holocaust and the birth of Israel displayed at least an overtly tribal self-affirmation. On the map of the Middle East there was a place for this tribe, even if millions of its members were in America. This map and land signaled a sense of worth. Americans of all faiths adopted much of the language of Israel, thinking of their nation as chosen and covenanted, a collection of tribes or itself a tribe among the nations—in Abraham Lincoln's term, an "almost chosen people."

For academics, tribes also meant the units that anthropologists study. Once upon a time people named primitives seemed fair game only for missionaries and agents of technology, said critics, who intruded and overturned their ways of life. Some of the primitives could defend themselves with spears or blowguns, but in recent decades anthropologists became their defenders against missionaries and technologues. In the process they often romanticized the value of such tribes over against the roughshod ways of those who would do away with their cultures. Sometimes they neglected to notice the fact that many tribespeople chose the mixed blessings of education, clinics, and machinery in order to live longer and more satisfying lives. In any case, during the twilight years the scholars who studied them did succeed in showing the values of the tribe to previously unthinking moderns.

If the last of these examples are far away and disappearing people, tools for observation of tribes turn up their moral counterparts close by. Some scholars have twitted their colleagues by looking at the academy as made up of tribes or as constituting a single tribe. The academy lives by myths, including one that says that academic tenure is an ultimate value needed for protecting academic freedom. Faculty members are as conscious of their place in the hierarchy from instructor to senior professor as are priests from curate to cardinal. Faculty members may be diffident and even uneasy about robes and processions, but the rites of which they are a part survive or reappear soon after iconoclasts try to extinguish them. The academic tribe decides its values, too. For some purposes of inquiry, discovery, and debate, one can say of it what Robert Hutchins said of his single university: not very good, but simply the best there is.

The family-in-context, not the nuclear family as such, still bears some marks of the tribe. With wearying frequency analysts tell how the extended family has disintegrated, and in many ways it has. But many thoughtful people recognize that they inherited more than genes along with their family membership. With them also came distinctive ways of doing things or thinking them, customs and manners, stories and hopes. The family network is one of the littlest of the little platoons. When connected in networks of relationships or with other families, it can still provide some elements of the tribe. Realistically, however, most observers picture it by itself as being almost defenseless or, at the very least, in need of other kinds of support.

In this context appear the religious communities, be they congregations, church movements, or church bodies. After a period at midcentury in which congregations were losing their rationales and church bodies were expected to adopt a homogenizing ecumenical ideal, expectations changed. People dug in to their congregations and favored these over their regional jurisdictions. These regional bonds were more important than denominations. Soon it was even possible to speak of a new denominationalism, as people gave more loyalty to their separate church bodies than to the more vague and impersonal church universal. All these moves make it possible to see the church as a tribe. For eighth-generation loyalists in a particular group this vision is no surprise. But converts also quickly adopt the thought patterns and gestures of their newly acquired religious community. A convert to higher Anglicanism, for example, is likely to be most vocal in opposition to changes in the Prayer Book and may soon acquire the kind of accent needed for the proper intonation of psalms or praying of collects on the soil of Canterbury.

For centers of meaning and belonging, the local church has had the greatest appeal, and in congregational context the tribal loyalties most readily emerged. Lord James Bryce, a nineteenth-century British ambassador to the United States, once remarked that the distinctive feature of tribal deities is that they are a means of interpreting one's local setting. So the tribal deity of the congregation stands in the way of universal appeals or prophetic charges. Not all local churches welcome new participants, find it easy to integrate them, or adopt any aspect of their vision. As strangers the newcomers may interrupt the serenity and coziness of revered ways of thinking and acting.

Some positive emphases counter the negative features of such tribal expressions. In a world of upsetting change, tribes or their surrogates can at least indicate hints of continuity. Through the churches some sort of tradition can live. Moderns are thus able to recognize that others before them have been tested and have remained loyal. The church provides a repository of options for a judging and saving people, because in its lore and among the people who make it up there is a believable word that was once spoken to people in other circumstances than their own. In the church the possibility of mutual support and bonding, so needed in an impersonal world, lives on. And because the church sees itself as being open to a transcendent word, it always has the potential of feeding the deepest motives in life and moving people toward self-sacrifice and the love of others.

Forces that compromise the church as a tribe are also evident. Most obvious is its voluntary character. People are aware thay they can choose a particular church, reject all churches, or switch between them should one or another inconvenience participants or challenge their cherished ways of life. For these reasons, particularly where religious forces are unarmed in free societies, they are relatively impotent for those of truly tribal instincts. Such people tend to turn to still another center of influence, one to which we have already alluded by reference to Native Americans, blacks and Jews, but which one can extend indefinitely: race, ethnic group, or nation.

A quarter century after the birth of the United Nations and the World Council of Churches, only decades after United World Federalism was an ideal, and but years after the images of "spaceship earth" and "the global village" seemed plausible, it was clear that a countering reality had undercut them. To paraphrase Harold Isaacs, all over the world one could see a "massive, convulsive ingathering of peoples." They created new separatenesses or over-againstnesses on the soil of old but almost forgotten commitments. They used these separatenesses to hold their own place or to assert their pride. Over against them were competing tribes which, it was feared, would displace their own. These tribes tended to carry a religio-cultural-ethnic cast, but all these were most potent when they linked up with the nation and the modern ideologies of nationalism.

The ethnic group or racial force was a biological entity. It drew potency from the fact that one came to it by blood. One could not really join the racial tribe. But the nation was different. One could emigrate to it, take out papers in it, and thus project loyalty to it. The state can raise armies, tax, and in other ways coerce assent. For these reasons it has needed the strenuous support of stories, rites, myths, ceremonies for reinforcement. Poet William Butler Yeats has said that one cannot grasp the universe bare-handed. For most people in our time, the nation best serves as a glove for the grasping. Some prophets predict that in the twenty-first century, religious or quasi-religious lines will provide the most efficient base for separateness among militants. Late in the twentieth the nation still serves to inform identity and inspire overagainstness. This is evident when one looks at the lethal rivalries between the USSR and China as nations despite their common commitment to communism, or between Arab states despite their uniting ethos derived from Islam.

Tribes offer at least four attractive features, beginning with identity. Who am I? If I am someone who owns no name and no group, I may be merely selfish or, worse, dangerous. Of course, the search for a personal identity on the part of someone who goes to the desert and there holds up a mirror to the self without reference to others may be a fad or a luxury. But a social identity is necessary for anyone who wishes to be of use to others, learning who one is in reference to a group. Erik Erikson urges that awareness of identity is necessary so that something in me can connect with something in you. Then continuity and the basis for trust will emerge. When persons come into wholly foreign circumstances they hear no recognizable language and do not know whether they are among horse thieves or nobles. They do not know how to act. Where there is a common language and set of manners based on tribal trust, they can respond creatively.

Second, the tribe allows for affection. Of course, there are and always will be internal rivalries in the tribe. But these become secondary when an external assault comes. In the ancient world, the residents of the isle of Crete were famous for their disputes with one another but more famous for the bonds they found whenever outside attackers came. Modern studies of the Orthodox synagogue find the participants engaged in what often seems to be cruel and derisive humor extended to other members of the group. But close-up analysis finds that this humor is a bonding agent. Let an outsider come and try to take up this form of expression and he will soon be invited or hounded out. People may not often think of the role of affection in the tribe. We have already seen how Thomas Jefferson did in his vision of the new nation. Later Americans might smile at his naivete, since their crowding and their internal pluralism have made such affection difficult to express. But whoever has felt the warmth of a good club or congregation, the strength of a trusting family or a believable nation, will recognize the dimensions of friendship and affection that enliven them.

Third, an aesthetic aspect marks modern tribal life. British social philosopher Ernest Gellner has rightly pointed out that once a tradition of a tribe has been broken, the people can never go home again to exactly the old ways. Gellner cites the medieval Muslim thinker Al-Ghazzali to the effect that people cannot be traditionalists once they are intimately aware of other traditions. From then on, they can only consciously readopt elements of the tribal tradition. On such terms, uprooted intellectuals reacquire the menus and names, the stories and heraldry of their distanced tribes. Subsequently, they often are more fanatic about them than are people who live unreflectively in protected social contexts. Gellner reminds us that such ethnic recoveries are not the stuff of life but only its decor. This is true, but whoever has an esthetic sensibility and grants a value to beauty in life will not sneer at decor. If my life has had no points of reference in a group, I can learn to respond to the hymnody or national anthems of an adopted tribe. For example, I am no one because I lacked a tradition. Life becomes more rich when I learn to speak of the Catholic way as "mine" or "ours," and to acquire rites that seemed to come as a birthright to others.

Somewhere along the way for most people on the journey there is a call to family experience through the movement of generations. The public church encourages this, for its little platoons of churches include littler platoons of families. What people call the monogamous nuclear family is not the day-to-day experience of all the people on the journey. Church life which acts as if it is will fail to reach most people. There is a single adult for every adult married couple in America. One third of the people over twenty-one need to be ministered to and to minister as singles. Sermons directed to the "traditional family" with father as breadwinner, mother as stay-at-home homemaker, both parents present in an intact marriage, and children under roof, would hit about one-fourteenth of the people. But most people somewhere along the way do have family experience or surrogates for it, so this most intimate social form relates to the congregational communities.

The public church looks to right and left and sees easier styles of family existence. To the right are more norm-bound and protected forms of religious life, whether in fundamentalist or conservative Catholic styles. In them every change evokes portrayal of all alternatives to the traditional family as the product of Satan and the humanists. But even in that quarter, stresses on marriage and family are intense. Celebrity evangelists often make news through the breakdowns in their own marriages and families, and divorce plagues the circles of legalist Catholics as well. Yet, they can argue that at least they do provide shelter from erosions that the more exposed communities in the public church cannot.

On the left, this churchly cluster also sees a prevalent but not more satisfying pattern. In the culture shaped by the media, by *People* magazine, television serials, and in the images of the Beautiful People, marriage and family are accidental stages along the way of life for some. Their arrangements are ad hoc, they make openly partial and temporary commitments, their fidelity is of the moment, and they go elsewhere for their stimulation. Never does a hint of a sacramental outlook enter the marriage relation. A vow is an inherited formality, not voluntary and solemn pledging of life so someone else can count on it.

The public church steers between these courses at a time when models and patterns for an alternative way are few. Its experts in the field know that the family cannot stand the pressure society exerts on it to be the shaper and transmitter of intimate values. It seldom gets a chance to do this because of the way it is surrounded by competitors in a world of media and public exposure. The few chances it does get are brief. The family can be compared to an evanescent art form, like the ballet. A curtain rises with the lights, and the curtain and the lights soon after drop again, a moment—probably twenty years—later. The tribe, not the family, says Rosenstock-Huessy, is the *couche*, the matrix of values. The so-called nuclear family can during its brief moment grasp and transmit these while making its contribution to the tribe, but it needs help. The public church, not being tribalist, does not find it easy to provide support.

The family has difficulty being a center of morale. The public church is that sector of American Christianity which provides a home for the more ardent advocates of fulfilling roles for women. The evangelical feminists are in its sphere, while their counterparts who favor models of submission seek the cover of more self-enclosed fundamentalisms. The mainline Protestants have long heard, if they have not yet fully heeded, the voice of their feminist members. And the Catholics who seek ordination of women and other realizations of female potential are not to be found in the ghettos of Roman traditionalism. All this means that the public church will acutely feel the strains upon marriage.

The self-enclosed churches provide their own sex and marriage manuals, their own magazines and novels and self-help lore, their own weekend seminars for expounding the ethos of the family. The public church, while making such materials and experiences available, does not shield its participants from ranging more widely. Thus non-Christian interpretations confuse participants even while they inform. Having said all this, however, one may note that something like the tribe does live on in the public church to provide values.

Countless of its familes *do* work, sacramentally and gracefully and without threat of hell or the promise of a cocoon.

The modern Christian family cannot function unless it becomes a spiritual center, a generator of morale. This it can hardly do if people under one roof have to carry the whole burden of nurture. Suppose members of a family do pick up biblical norms and visions for their life together and want to enhance them. In the case of mainline Protestants, for example, they may set out to observe the liturgical church year in the decor and rhythms of the home. The children, seeing this practice unconfirmed in any families of their acquaintance, will consider it to be an eccentricity of two parents, something so arcane that it never becomes part of their life.

Somehow the public church has to become conscious about providing something of the tribal experience if it is to generate the values. In an era of zero population growth, this obviously does not mean that its families can themselves grow large enough to form communities. In a time of mobility, these restless small nuclear families will not sit still long enough for second and third generations to live in proximity to the uncles and aunts of a first generation. Foster care can open some families. Extending them in other ways, through adoption, international student visits, taking in strays, borrowing, or whatever, will supplement still more. But families need more help.

The public church can extend its purposes by creating a social form larger than the family but smaller than the congregation, a sort of collegial family. The nuclear groups are colleagues to one another. They covenant and associate with one another in *collegia*. This term which has a medieval ring, connotes guilds of committed people. Properly so: collegial families within or across congregational lines provide explicit or strong if still tacit agreements to one another. Sometimes where there is baptism of infants, the families of godparents and godchildren form networks. Adults whose young people come of age at the same time in church school and youth movements come together. What has hitherto been done accidentally and occasionally now comes to be a calculated provision of the church.

The families as *collegia* make possible the transmitting of church tradition and the deliberation of values colored by it. Where we have seen them effective, these circles of more-than-friendship may undertake joint camping experiences. A young adolescent who cannot communicate with her parents might spend a weekend with parents in another unit of the collegial family. The unrelated children become cousins-by-choice. There are opportunities for intergenerational bonding, as people well past child-rearing years find a second round of influence. This is not the place to describe in detail such a form or to discuss the limits of it as an ideal type, but only to illustrate how the concept of a community of communities operates on mass and intimate levels alike, as support for the spiritual journey.

Many tribes, finally, carry in their lore something that can lead them to self-transcendence. The myths that give birth and life to tribes often give evidence of having a universal impulse. One never knows at which moment the force of that constituting myth will again hit a group. Thus in the rise of Israel there were prophetic passages like those in the book of Amos. While affirming that Israel was chosen, these lines also remind the people that Yahweh is the Lord of history. Yahweh has plans for and guides *other* nations as well. The original Christian stories are full of chastisements by Jesus of the disciples. In the Gospel of Mark, for instance, not once are they allowed to look good, because they want to find a way around the cross instead of to follow the way of the cross.

Sociologist Max Weber showed the difference between two types of leaders through two simple phrases. The charismatic leader—one is almost tempted to say the messiah only—can say, "It is written, but I say unto you." The religious virtuoso in a tradition can say, "It is written, *and I insist.*" A word spoken when the tribe was constituted may still be ahead of the group. It remains to be recovered and heard, as a step *beyond* the tribe that encased the original word and no longer hears it.

In sum, without the tribe, the person feels to be nothing. With the tribe and nothing but the tribe, the participant may be dangerous, for barbarianism comes with devotion to idols of the tribe. So the tribe needs a context, which in the language of myth and history alike, the city, the polis, the sphere of political interaction, represents.

8

Commitment Versus Civility

From the viewpoint of the polis, people who have only their tribe
to depend upon live apart. They huddle together, worship their local
deities, and display a kind of solipsism in which they talk in a language they alone can understand because it takes rise from thoughts
that cannot belong to any other group than theirs. The first mark of
such inverted tribes is exclusivism and belligerence, elements that
have become so obvious that they hardly need documentation.

A free society has room for a number of exclusive and belligerent
religious tribes. They have rights assured by the republic. So long as
there is a republic, there will be restraints against their being at one
another's throats. Eruptions of militant tribalism on the scale of the
Jonestown tragedy are always potentially present, but these have
been rare and on Jonestown's scale are unmatched in modern republican life. More frequently, tribal standoffishness is of an apparently
harmless sort. Most Americans find the Amish, the Old Order Men-
nonites, and the Hutterites to be quaint, not dangerous. In times of
war when they refuse military service people do resent and even
persecute them. How can there be a republic, it is asked, if people
refuse to serve in the military or support war efforts? Nonmembers of
their communities who live near them, however, do not always find
them quaint. Often such rural communal groups are an economic
inconvenience. They buy up land instead of the wares of village
merchants. They live off the economy but not really in it. Still, their
numbers are small and they live as a luxury in the back of the minds
of more interactive follow citizens.

The new tribalism that is an assault on the human city has come from larger religious groups that live in its midst but are reactive against it. They represent the first of two main personality types that psychoanalyst J. Robert Lifton has observed in our modern chaos. The one is protean, named after the god Proteus, who could assume any form. Every day he could be something else. So it is that some moderns show adaptive capacities that make it possible for their antennae to be out for every signal, their blotters and sponges available to absorb the most contradictory notions. But another type of people, who are equally cut off from tradition and continuity, react by developing constrictive personalities. They close themselves off. In the midst of the modern blur and flow, religious groups that appeal to the constrictive type prosper.

A National Council of Churches lawyer, Dean M. Kelley, set the theme for church analysis in the 1970s with a book on the growth of more constrictive churches and on the relative decline of more open ones. On one page Kelley worked out a gradient which showed that the more open a church was, the less it prospered as an agency to attract new converts. The more constrictive and closed it was, the more likely it was to grow. Such growth did occur under relatively low ceilings, and within limits. Only a certain number of American millions had the problems to which these churches' solutions appealed. But under that ceiling they did make impressive gains.

The norms by which they lived, noted Kelley, included features that we associate less with tribes than with tribal*ism*. The tribe can afford to be a bit relaxed, but to ward off the assaults of modernity, the tribalist has to be an absolutist. No one outside the group possesses anything like the truth. Tribalists, Kelley went on, had to be fanatic, zealous, compulsively missionary, incapable of hearing because they insisted on speaking, and the like. Some leaders of mainline churches later used Kelley as a manual of arms. They reasoned that they might do well to be *a little bit* absolutist, *reasonably* fanatic, *sensibly* zealous, *more or less* missionary, and *a little* less open to the word of others. Their efforts to play catch-up ball were unconvincing because they rose more from a sense of strategy than conviction. Prospective converts who desire absolutism and fanaticism know where they want to be attracted. Any group that hints at compromise will be unappealing.

On the list of church bodies that grew most because they were most closed were groups that include many fine citizens. But what they have in common is the absence of anything in common, any elements that might make interaction, minimal consensus, a public philosophy, or a republic possible. At the head of that list, for instance, were Orthodox Jews and Black Muslims. Try as people may for weeks on end, it is not likely that they will find any basis for commonality between them. Their members have different concepts of God, of human origins and destiny, of their chosenness, and of legitimate ways for them to live up to the norms of their faith.

Suppose one could get the two of them to talk to each other. How would a third party enter, if it comes from the upper end of Kelley's growing-because-closed gradient? For another group is the Jehovah's Witnesses. Again, the Witnesses may be sacrificial people. Their steadfastness against Soviet oppression is admirable. They may shame halfhearted adherents of other religious bodies because of their steadfastness. But no one is more ready than a member of the Jehovah's Witnesses to say that they accept nothing, not one thing, in the ministry of other religious groups. The other groups are under the rule of Satan, as are all earthly civil societies including that of the United States of America. Even in intimate matters like health care, the Jehovah's Witnesses stand apart. They refuse to permit the blood transfusion of a child even if death results from their stand. But if we would see them drawn into the republic of the closed-off tribes, how can one integrate them with Christian Science, which was next on Kelley's lists? Christian Scientists tend to be patriotic Americans, often in the mainstream of life, and they are genial enough. But their cognitive system matches that of none of the other groups. To conceive of them in an *una sancta catholica* next to the Witnesses is impossible.

Over against all these in the top seven are the Churches of Christ, who are biblical fundamentalists, restorationists, who feel that all other churches are false, or partly false, because they are not literalist about New Testament norms. One expects to hear the most vehement criticism of Jehovah's Witnesses from members of the Churches of Christ. Far milder are the Seventh-Day Adventists, whom many see moving toward the evangelical mainstream. Their rejection of Sunday worship carried vehement anti-Catholic tones, but their defense of Saturday worship has helped win liberties for others. They are specialists in support of the First Amendment to the Constitution. But their level of acceptance of other Christians is not high. Also in the top growth-group are the Latter-Day Saints. Today these Mormons are true-blue Americans, adherents of the conservative American way of life. Yet their history takes rise from a movement of judgment against that way, which was an effort to colonize a kingdom apart from the norms of the United States. More than a century ago they had their own armies and were at war with the United States. During their transit to statehood, most often citizens rejected their church as theocratically dangerous and polygynously immoral. Thoroughly respectable now, they still throw fear into many non-Mormons, and their religious outlook at almost no point matches that of those who call themselves orthodox.

Kelley also included evangelical and pentecostal churches, few of which would have anything to do with any of the groups mentioned here. But we will pursue their separate and varied stories elsewhere and note them now only to say that together they provide or show no means for developing an ecumenical religious reality or a true republic with the others. Some of them are thoroughly involved with the life of the human city in an open engagement. Others produce Christian Yellow Pages and vote only for their fellow Born Agains as a sign of tribal standoffishness.

While exclusiveness and belligerence may be the main mark of these tribes, it is clear from the above account that they generate a minority outlook. Of course, every American religious group does when measured against any universalizing ideal. There may be 50,000,000 Catholics, but they are a minority in respect to the content of their creed since almost none of the other 175,000,000 Americans are obedient to the Roman pope. Baptists may be an enormous body, yet their view of believers' baptism is a window on a world of doctrines that separate them from others. There seems to be little basis for group loyalty when there is no cognitive difference between members and nonmembers. Sociologist Robert Bellah has urged that Americans, who have been overinfluenced by the outlook of doctrinal Christianity, should rejoin the human race by minimizing the substance of *belief* in religion. But if they did so formally, there would still be cognitive differences based on world views and fundamental grasps of reality even if no creed were in sight.

So each tribe regards itself as a cognitive minority; but the tribal*ists* build a wall around their circle of cognition and those who share life in it. Tribal solipsism results. Needless to say, this impulse is not a monopoly of tight and right religious groups. Some black theologians have argued not merely that one must be a black to write theology for blacks, but that since theology is the preserve of the oppressed and they are the normatively oppressed group, no one who is not a black can write theology at all. There have been feminist theologians who have argued not merely that one must be a woman to write theology for women but that since theology is the preserve of the once-dominated, now liberated, and, since they are the cohort that fits such terms, no one who is not a woman can write theology at all. Some advocates of liberation theology use similar language about

Third World peoples, but then go on to claim adoption into Third World tribes or the adoption of Third World mentalities. Some charismatic Christians disavow all who have not had "the experience" and they disallow the Christian character of expression on the part of noncharismatics. What is distinctive about these narrow minorities, then, is not the fact that they have particular beliefs and that only they hold them, but that they reject as invalid all efforts by others to give expression to fundamental human reality. Humane discourse breaks down before it starts, and theological empathy is not conceivable at all. There can be no city, but only tribes on their separate turfs.

A third mark of the tribalist mentality is its generally messianic, millennial, and often prophetically utopian tinge. I use those three marks formally and not by reference to content. They may not all hold a literalistic view of a millennial or one thousand-year reign of Christ. They may not all look for the messiah. They may not all believe that within history there can be a community in which everything turns out all right for everyone. What they do succeed in representing is the notion that they possess the secret of history and have a monopoly on it. They are convinced that the trajectory of their group is the only one that offers both a saving faith for eternal issues and an ordering faith for human existence. This stance leads them to a generally negative valuation of human endeavor. People are to find meaning in life only by signing up with them and their leader. Adherents are to belong to this tribe and dare not share loyalties with, say, political groups or voluntary associations.

Criticism of the tribes should be obvious and easy. At many moments in the life of the republic it has been apt and telling. Curiously, today one must defend the right to criticize. In a world of doubt and half belief, even the most belligerent groups receive admiration from people who have nothing in common with their members. Indeed, the admirers would be the first targets for persecution should such groups prevail. Later we shall diagnose the impulse to affirm the negators, to admire the antirepublicans, and to envy those who have faith, any faith, so long as they hold to it fanatically. For now, some criticisms of them are in order.

First, they have their rights, but they do not all assure others their rights or care about them. Some of the church bodies in the list above, it must be said, do not belong in this category. Seventh-Day Adventists, for example, will serve as *amici curiae* for all kinds of non-Adventist cases in courts. But for most tribalist groups, there is contentment to live off the republic and off the guarantees of the city without any evidence of effort to enhance the values or assure the future of freedom.

What is more urgent about the new problem of the tribalism in America and around the world, rises from trends in demography and weaponry. In lightly populated primitive societies the tribes often wanted to be left alone. They might make minimally armed forays onto the territory of other tribes and return home with few casualties. But now the world is more crowded. All the way from West Bengal and Kerala, through Zaire, beyond Northern Ireland to California, they jostle one another. Little space separates them, so their militancy finds practical expression.

Modern weaponry makes tribalism more dangerous. Once upon a time, one could sulk in the hills and merely resent others in silence. Today a few dollars for plastique or grenades and a measure of the will to use them, coupled with the employment of mass media as instruments for publicity, make formerly passive people who opted out of the greater society now capable of holding it hostage. Any effort the larger society can expend to keep its citizens in the circle of republican discourse minimizes the lethal potential.

Of course, there are also resources in theology for criticism of the tribalist. Even the biblical literalist, who believes that there is no covenant to match that of "old" or "new" Israel and who affirms with a biblical writer that there is no other name than Jesus by which people will be saved, has to reckon with the expansive messages and glimpses in the Bible. Israel is also to be "a light to the nations." From Isaiah to Malachi there are glimpses of the way the Lord of Israel is the Lord of the nations. Israel's eschatology, its language about the end-time and what follows it, has a bearing on the people who are not of Israel.

The New Testament frequently endows with value people who are not of the elect group. The Gospel writers portray Jesus finding faith in the heart of Roman centurions who were not of the covenant, or applauding the Syro-Phoenician foreigner, while he called his chosen disciples victims of Satan who serve demonic purposes. The apostle Paul boasted of being of "no mean city" as a Roman. In his Letter to the Romans he legitimated the Roman city and its government as being ordained of God. While Christians were a cognitive minority, their Christ had a cosmic bearing, and "in him all things hold together." If only one of ten lepers came back to praise God, yet the divine power in the name of Jesus could heal all ten. While the eschatological passages envision a new Jerusalem to replace the human city and while many of the first believers were taken up with its vision, they also were and were to be responsible participants in the Roman orbit.

As for today, because they do believe that "all things cohere in Christ," the components of the public church may look like a single tribe in relation to militants on their own left and right in Christianity, to participants in non-Christian faiths, and to people of secular outlook, with whom they share concern for the human city. They make up the religious groups that Benjamin Franklin in his call for a "public religion" was sure could make a contribution to public virtue and the commonweal. Observers of this public religion expect such Christians not only to interact among themselves but also to build on common appeals to reason and humaneness for the ordering of the human city. For these tasks the public church *symbiotes* live with distinction between what we might call "saving faith," which enlivens each tribe, and "ordering faith," which these tribes and nonbelievers can share. Saving faith calls for a particular story and a communal language. The ordering faith or ordering *logos* sees God active even where people are not in the process of being reconciled, only of being governed and governing.

The values of the city are twisted and distorted, for the city lives under the mark of death and human stain. But God works also through those values, for the better ordering of justice. The *symbiotes* learn from each other how to contribute to this ordering. Roman Catholics and Baptists, for example, revise their outlooks on creeds and freedoms by seeing how these are prismed through the experience of each other's church. They learn through these exposures that none of their tribes, nor all of them taken together, have a monopoly on humane values or social truth.

If a note of defensiveness mixed with urgency and tinged with despair appears in this defense of the larger community, and if it displays a weariness over having to rehearse support of the city once more, these result from a reading of contemporary culture. The signs of the times show little support for public faith or civility in religion. Why are there losses of faith? What can be done to resurrect them or replace such faith with an equivalent?

In our half-believing age nostalgia grows for the days people presume to have been ages of faith. Back when there were cathedrals and crusades, *then* no one shilly-shallied or had doubts about identity or hopes. Then they *really* believed enough to chase the infidel from holy places. The mind recalls crusaders' crosses and crusaders' hymns, stalwart men with red crosses, soldiers riding white horses to vindicate God against the enemy. Fortunately, or unfortunately, our minds have buried the recall of contemporary accounts: of how the merciful men of faith immediately killed the children of Jerusalem while the less merciful ones tortured the infidel. Blood, said Raymond of Agiles, was so deep that it reached the knees of horses, and the horses slipped in it. But, he went on, it was all a glorious judgment of God against people who had profaned the holy places.

On those terms, Americans remember when their ancestors were absolutist and fanatic, zealous and missionary, not given to relativism, dialogue, or doubt. Columbus himself sold the exploration of Western waters to Iberian royalty as part of a continuing crusade. The round globe allowed him, in the name of Catholic Castile and Aragon, to come at the Turk from the back, to stab him there—with weapons paid for by trade with or plunder from Cathay, en route. Columbus himself seemed civil when he confronted the Native Americans that he called Indians, for "they invite you to share anything that they possess, and show as much love as if their hearts went into it." But he was also uncivil enough to say "they have no religion," and incivil enough to say "how easy it would be . . . to make them work for us," which meant to enslave them.

The ancestors of mainline and evangelical Protestants also were not compromised by civility. When Menendez de Aviles at Saint Augustine, Florida, massacred all of the Protestant Huguenot colony nearby, he was careful not to transplant his motives to the politics of Europe. Incivility worked best in religion. He explained his killings: "Done, not as to Frenchmen but as to Lutherans." Three years later Dominique de Gourgues, vindicating the French, also kept away from civil politics: "Done not as to Spaniards, but as to murderers and thieves."

When the New Englanders came they were sure of their faith and unmindful of the roots of faith in others. No one who was not of their tribe need come closer than the harbor. Tolerant Rhode Island they called the *latrina* of New England. One among them looked back ruefully at the growth of tolerance in old England. Fancying himself a humorist, Nathaniel Ward, "the simple cobbler of Aggawam" derided the civil style: "He that is willing to tolerate any religion, or discrepant way of religion, besides his own, unless it be in matters merely indifferent, either doubts of his own, or is not sincere in it." With those words he sounded like the admirer of tribalism in an age of compromised faith.

In New Amsterdam Governor Peter Stuyvesant resented the pressure old Amsterdam put on him to welcome Jews in 1654. They were good cosmopolitan traders. Jews were on the sponsoring board in the Netherlands and the Netherlands had seen the birth of tolerance, so he had to allow Jews to settle. In the finest "dammit, there goes the neighborhood" spirit the Governor complained. If he had to take Jews, soon he would find no grounds for keeping out the Lutherans and the Catholics. Even benign and enlightened Benjamin Franklin did not want to accept "the Palatine boors" of Lutheranism to his own reasonable Pennsylvania, because they might Germanize everyone else before they were "Englished" themselves. The tribes even in his view could not mix.

Later Americans learned that they had no alternative but to invent patterns of life to minimize conflict. The denominational system allowed each tribe to keep its convictions intact, while it worked to channel their impulses toward conflict into harmless passages. Competition remained vicious but was rarely bloody. Baptist and Methodist revivalists battled against leftover Episcopalians on the frontier, but all three of them could unite against the new Disciples of Christ and all four of them against the Catholics. In Philadelphia and Boston Protestant tribespeople burned some convents and killed a few Irish Catholic members of tribes. There was a "Mormon Meadows Massacre" in the west. But clearly the age of faith was ending, say the nostalgic, as tolerance and mutual acceptance grew. Two types of civil religion developed as a result. One was the overarching national type that made the separate tribes irrelevant or that removed their reasons to persecute each other. The other was a movement toward civil religion in the sense that the values of civility, of the city, compromised those of the tribe. A new etiquette prevailed.

By 1980, who was there left to admire? Those envious of incivil commitment celebrated it among some of the young people who joined what the media insisted on calling cults. While their contemporaries were laid back, getting their MBA degrees or sniffing cocaine, these people got themselves together and surrendered everything for faith in their leaders and their new familial tribes. From the advance guard in mainline Protestantism and selected secular sources one began to hear more than grudging acclaim. Never matter what the devotees believed in, or what the belief did to their minds. These adherents, we were told, were like the early Christians, zealous and cutthroat, unheeding and uncompromising. They were a judgment on the open-minded churches, which did not provide enough authoritarianism.

Who else was left to admire? The Jewish Defense League or the Gush Emunim in Israel, which would kill for conviction. Muslim militants, until those in Iran began to inconvenience America, and even there the demodernizing impulse won praise by half believers who either yearned for a faith, any faith, or taunted other modern believers who would not kill in the name of faith. Some admired the militant fundamentalists, feeling that they would not prevail, but using their frozen faith as a norm to measure all developing types.

The Enlightenment spirit is now in eclipse, whether or not the age of civility is dying, only to be replaced by mere tribalism where the tribes cancel or kill each other, or by totalist faiths that coerce conviction on whole populations. Yet the more onimous trend may not be the increase of incivility—most citizens do not yet worry about that or seem aware of it; and, in any case, how does one measure it—but *the decrease of faith in civility.* The spiritual void that produces a yearning for faith no matter what its object, or an awe for people of conviction no matter what their convictions, is a late twentieth-century innovation.

Sometimes taunts against civility come from those who consider themselves to be outside the circle of all faiths. An anthology of this sort of derision is available in any dictionary of quotations on tolerance. The lines are telling enough to sting. Bertrand Russell: "Religious toleration, to a certain extent, has been increasing because people have ceased to consider religion so important as it was once thought to be." Arnold Lunn: "Mutual toleration of religious views is the product not of faith but of doubt." Will Durant: "Tolerance grows only when faith loses certainty; certainty is murderous."

In such readings the observers fail to do much psychological probing. When people in the midst of pluralism spend their energies building psychic walls around themselves, could it be that their faith is little more than what C. J. Jung called "overcompensated doubt"? More significantly, these critics of civility tend to display both historical and theological naivete. They have been convinced by twentieth-century fundamentalists of a proposition few historians of Jewish or Christian faith would ever agree to: that orthodox faith shows no development. They take to themselves the task of describing what was and is normative Western faith. Ordinarily it turns out to be not the historic catholic traditions of Israel or Christianity, but the repressive faith they rejected from their parents or neighbors in their adolescent years. The historian can show, for example, how the Protestant fundamentalism of 1925 was a very modern invention, a reaction against a modern challenge. It drew on some ancient Christian themes and fused them with Baconian philosophy and Common Sense Realism mediated through nineteenth-century Princeton Seminary. They claimed that what they came up with was fundamental Christianity, though their views of the millennium had known few witnesses through all the Christian centuries. And historic

Catholic Christians would never have agreed that a movement like fundamentalism, which slighted baptism and the eucharist and found them irrelevant as part of the common treasure of affirmations, dared claim a monopoly on historic faith. But this fundamentalism had prevailed as the totality of Christianity in the town in Tennessee "up from whose slavery" selected humanists had risen. They used that particular version of the faith as the standard for measuring who believed and who did not. They found such defining most convenient since this kind of faith held no lures or challenges for them. In the process they made no room for or gave no hearing to believers who were aware of Christian development, disciples of Christ who believed that faith and interpretation belong together, members who felt no impulses to compensate for their doubts by engaging in fanaticism or crusades.

My anthology of taunts against tolerance also includes derision from within the Christian community. Again, its sayings sting. G. K. Chesteron: "Toleration is the virtue of people who do not believe anything." Father Robert Gannon: "Tolerance . . . is the lowest form of human cooperation. It is the drab, uncomfortable, halfway house between hate and charity." On those terms, fundamentalists attacked moderate evangelicals like Billy Graham for his symbiotic relations and shared platforms with mainline Protestants and evangelical Roman Catholics. In the same spirit Archbishop Marcel Lefebvre set out to attack the popes for compromising through their support of the Second Vatican Council's revisions and the Council's friendly view of non-Catholic Christianity, Judaism, and world religions. And in the same spirit the Gush Emunim or "bloc of the faithful" named itself the only true reader of the Hebrew Scriptures because it insisted, against the will of even the Israeli majority, on creating antagonisms on the West Bank.

The humanist and Christian critics of tolerance in religion carried the spirit of animus against civility over into admiration of the more intolerant parties within denominations as they went about their warfare. Those Episcopalians and other Catholic believers who favor the ordination of women acted out of profound conviction and on the basis of refined critical theology, but the fundamentalist-minded humanists decided that the intransigent faction was the party of conviction, never of overcompensated doubt. Protestants who abhorred and saw as demonic the Catholic declaration of papal infallibility in 1870 produced heirs who admired the pope for cracking down in the name of infallibility on thinkers who called it into question on traditional and historic grounds.

These sudden enthusiasms for papal infallibilist style on the part of belligerent Protestants and of Protestant scriptural inerrancy on the part of dogmatic Catholics introduced confusion to the scene. Those who were suddenly enthusiastic were the heirs of parties which once upon a time had resisted the *content* of doctrines whose *form* they now so admire. Once upon a time it was the scriptural inerrancy people in Protestantism who were most shocked when papal infallibility was proclaimed. And the infallibilist party historically had least appreciation for the "Bible alone" claims of the Protestant inerrantists. Infallibility was proclaimed in 1870, at about the same time as inerrancy was being devised. In both cases, these were more efficient as weapons to be wielded than as guardians of faith. Also in both cases they produced awe and admiration among those who are uneasy with civility in religion.

This review has been a plea for a more catholic historical sense. It has not been a defense of tolerance. The Bertrand Russells and the G. K. Chestertons are correct to criticize the pallid character of tolerance in religion. The alternative to fanaticism need not be passive tolerance, it can be passionate commitment. A wearied and wary novelist, Herman Melville, stated the terms for this: "But when a man's religion becomes really frantic; when it is a positive torment to him; and, in time, makes this earth of ours an uncomfortable inn to lodge in; then I think it high time to take that individual aside and argue the point with him."

Arguing the point grows from not one but two convictions: the first is to the content of an alternate view of what faith is and the second is to the integrity of the faith of people with whom one disagrees. Tolerance holds to neither, since it ordinarily suggests that belief does not matter and that one must hold lightly to faith if one is to make room for the belief of others. This would be the most disastrous kind of outlook for people of real faith. One can turn this notion around and say that what the world needs is more faithful commitment, not less, than the kind fanatic fundamentalists or Christian crusaders advocate or exemplify. How can one be sure that they are not acting to defend the boundaries of the tribe only because they lack a real core of faith? How can one be sure that they are not walling in their psyche because there is a void at the center?

Fanaticisms, including twentieth-century totalitarianisms, grow on the soil of those who lack conviction, until the worst, filled with passionate intensity, take them over. People who live in a culture of *anomie,* normlessness, fall victim to the assertions of every kind of norm. Victims of *accedia,* the inability to affirm in the face of spiritual good, are vacuums ready to be filled by the most potent pourers. To leave a spiritual void by touting weak faith or wan commitment in a

pluralist society is to invite the overcoming of pluralism by any dem-
agogue who has a convincing manner and promise.

If the world does not need more tolerance, it *does* need what
Gabriel Marcel has called, inelegantly but aptly, "counter-
intolerance." This takes the form of responsiveness to the convictions of people who believe differently than I, and an empathy for
what and why they believe, precisely because I believe so deeply
that I have been tempted to intolerance. I guarantee others complete
freedom to the extent that I hold to my opinion, says Marcel. I envis-
age the other doing the same, if I put myself in his place. "My
awareness of my own conviction is somehow my guarantee of the
worth of his." If I make moves to convince him of the truth of my
own, they can never be through force or deception, lest I seem "a
servant of a God of prey whose goal it is to annex and enslave." That,
he writes, is a loathsome image of God.

"A God of prey" is exactly the picture one gets from crusading
converters who allow for no integrity in the faith of others. Such a
God, one concludes, would annex and enslave, not convince and
persuade. And this God of our tribe would allow no other tribes to
encroach on our territory and would impel us to seek domain over
theirs. What is at stake in the loss of faith in civility, whether in the
political or the churchly realm, is the arrival of faith in such a licensing God of prey.

Some fairly cheerful things remain to be said in the face of the loss
of faith in civility. This book celebrates the survival of tribes of mainline Protestants, the emergence of open-evangelicals, and the transformations of Catholics who have learned "counter-intolerance."
The secular canopy over society, while itself no cover for a new
civility, at least contributes because it does not let all religious
people take themselves too seriously. The pluralism of the society
itself is one kind of guarantee so long as it remains rich since it is
then hard for a single crusading voice to prevail. Ecumenical and
interfaith movements may be in trouble, but their spirit somehow
expands nevertheless. There are great human models: Pope John
XXIII, Martin Luther King, Mohandas Gandhi, Abraham Joshua
Heschel, Dorothy Day, Dietrich Bonhoeffer, Thomas Merton, are
people who spent their lives ransacking their own particular traditions in line with their commitment to the universal. We think of
them as cosmopolitan, yet they remained faithful to their tradition en
route.

The theological program for counter-intolerance is only beginning
to be worked out. John Murray Cuddihy properly scorned the
henotheism that he thinks must stand behind all civility in religion.

Henotheism, over against monotheism, says in effect that there are as many gods as there are tribes. Members of a tribe allow the others to survive but do so in a spirit of "my god is better than your God." Mere polytheism, the idea that there is at least one god per tribe, but that there is no hierarchy among them, tempts others. But counting deities, whether in mono-, heno-, or polytheism, is a reductive way to go about the business of legitimating pluralism in a world where all other choices are less satisfying. One can believe in the God beyond the gods, the ultimate source of truth and value, the Ground of Being, Israel's one Lord, the God to whom Jesus was transparent and whom he embodied, and still see this God active beyond the story the Christian inherits. This God is active within the story beyond the saving task, ordering the universe, human governments, and humane endeavors. If God is present beyond the tribe, then the tribe engages in idolatry when its claims are in every way exclusive.

Determinists have made a law of history out of their parochial observations in parts of the West. They say that all growth of civility must mean decline of faith, that all spread of counter-intolerance means contraction of conviction. Yet many Buddhists have lived by the Decree of Asoka (264–228 B.C.E.): "It is forbidden to deny other sects; the true believer gives honor to whatever in them is worthy of honor." And such Buddhism lasted through the centuries. Many adherents of Hinduism have been affirmative of other ways without losing passion for their own. Many in Israel embraced the world and other faiths without losing their sense of chosenness and election. The God of prey is not alone in the pantheon.

The God who quickens faith but who need not annex and enslave has found witnesses and needs them. As a first step toward developing a theology and ethos that fuse civility and conviction, the public church as a communion of communions would do well to charter some case studies of the cells and tribes which through the years have stood against the crusading and fanatic grain. What made them tick? What picture of God sustained them? Did their heirs lose conviction more or less readily than do the children of zealots who worked themselves out of the repression that first ruled them? How did they articulate this faith?

Such people and movements have never been more than a minority in romantic ages of faith or realistic ages of half faith. The world, however, is now too crowded, too full of weapons and incendiary possibilities, to allow for the luxury of lost faith in civility. The most heroic task ahead for believers in the public church communions will be to bring their part of humanity to a whole new stage of faith, in which the God of prey is left behind and people can affirm what they believe without pouncing on others. Many observers envision that the twenty-first century, far from being merely secular, may be hyperreligious. They go on to say that potent human organization may no longer follow the lines of nations but the outlines of religions until great tribes, well armed, will clash. If that script is plausible, any efforts to invent a way to be civil by conviction and committed to civility are the mark of highest responsibility. The nonreligious citizenry can play only a small part in this invention, since it lacks a response to the sacred chords when these vibrate in the human story. Among the religious, including Christians, the public church, standing over against the totalist state religions, against merely private faith, or against tribalist churches, has an urgent calling.

9

Passivity Versus Action

The Christian faith calls people to be, before it calls them to be good. To be means for them to find themselves grounded in the care of God, transformed by the love of Christ, whole. To be good calls them to serve as the channels through which that love reaches others. The Christian faith is not first of all a system of universal morality or ethics, propagated as an ideal which Christians should impose on those who do not share their view of the New Creation. Some scholars can find only a trace or two of such a universal note in the setting of the Good Samaritan story or the Letter of James. Instead the message calls participants into the new life in Christ to live out of their own story, the story that discloses to them the power and being of God and their life in Christ.

These reminders are necessary because, in a free nation which makes room for voluntary churches, it is tempting for the society to legitimate the churches as mere generators of morality. They receive tax exemption because of services rendered the state. A suburban realtor advertises the presence of churches in a new community, both in order to show that there are conveniences for buyers and also to imply that it will be a good community. The churches, in return, have accepted the offer and advertised themselves as bearers of morality and propagators of a standard.

A further reason for reminding Christians and others of the limits of their scope is the temptation that grows when the society becomes so pluralistic that its majority does not live by the Christian story as the various story-tellers expound it.

Once upon a time, in a cozier colonial setting, the religious elites of communities set the terms for those communities. They provided the *nomos*, the legal standard, based on "the laws of Moses" or "the law of Christ." This standard, now regarded by many as foolishly repressive and dismissed with sneered versions of the term "Puritan," once produced good effect. People knew who they were, to what they belonged, and from what they deviated *if* they deviated. The outsider was not welcome. The stranger or sailor was confined to quarters in the harbor or on the ship. The wandering Jesuit was quietly given dinner and sent on his way, or he knew better in the first place than to wander to the colony in question. But strangers eventually came to stay and sailors settled in. Merchants deviated from the standard. "Immigrants" came with other stories, other standards. There were also later colonies that wanted to help form a single nation.

The new nation had to broaden the scope of the moral fabric, as both Christian law and an enlightened view of natural reason led to firm but diffuse calls for "public virtue." Before more than two decades passed, the Protestant revivalists, again propagating their own moral responses, overwhelmed the enlightened religion. For a long period Protestants worked to establish or reestablish a Christian civilization. They dreamed of the millennial age and wanted to make the world so attractive that Christ would reappear. Some of them advocated "disinterested benevolence," a pattern of love for God in Christ that issued in selfless concern for others. A network of reformist institutions grew as the moral churches in their righteous empire worked to eradicate intemperance, prostitution, profanity, and—in the case of the daring few—slavery. Where disinterested benevolence was not effective, these Christians reached for law. When they wavered in support of it, some of the later immigrants replaced them. British observer D. W. Brogan noted that as rural Protestantism slipped from legal Puritanism, urban and especially Irish Catholicism perpetuated it. There were Legions of Decency to boycott or shun immoral films, books, and the like.

For reasons too complicated to enlarge upon here, the pluralization of America further complicated the idea of a universal moral standard. Anthropologists kept coming back with reports to the sophisticates in the culture: there seemed to be no natural reason or natural law whose contents informed the consciences of *all* humanity. Everywhere there were tribes that violated what American Christians thought was written "into the hearts" (Romans 1) of Gentiles who "knew not the law" revealed to Moses or through Christ and the scriptures. This insight led to a sense of relativity: we can propagate our moral standards but can find no general ones to impose.

But who were the people who would say "our"? Half of America in the twentieth century was unchurched. This was the smallest percentage in history, but no longer could the churched minority count on the culture itself to promote its moral standards in legislatures, courts, schools, and the ethos. And the members of the churched half could not agree among themselves. Jews did not have one standard, but a rich variety of Orthodox, Conservative, and Reform standards. Secular humanists, despised by the religious right wing, often had another. They lived by the "public religion" of the republic or *A Common Faith* or *The Public Philosophy* of their John Deweys and Walter Lippmanns.

Within Christianity there were also visibly varied patterns. Catholics gave lip service, at least, to natural law and, until the 1960s, almost all of them said that this natural law forbade artificial birth control. Most Protestants had agreed with them, but the agreement came eighty years earlier and was no longer in effect. So in state after state, as Protestants revised their view of what was natural or artificial in family planning, they worked to take off the books the laws against birth control that they themselves had put there, and which Catholics now defended. Liberal and conservative Protestants, in a last-ditch effort to promote their moral system, succeeded in amending the Constitution to prohibit the sale and consumption of alcoholic beverages, a movement defied by most Catholics and many continental Protestants like the Lutherans. These may have shared the prohibitionists' concern against abuse but may never have included teetotalism in their program. The public perceived the division in the churchly ranks.

In the 1960s ecumenical and liberal Protestantism, along with its Catholic and Jewish counterparts, shared the progressivism and utopianism of many in the technological and political order. In their think tanks and with their task forces, their bureaucratic and intellectual leaders dreamed dreams of a secular city that Christians would somehow inform and find congenial. They linked up with propagators of the New Frontier or the Great Society and worked to eradicate evils like poverty, racial injustice, inequality, and war. They found company beyond politics and the academy among people of good will, or at least their kind of good will. If the polls were accurate, they never attracted a majority of their own fellow congregants to their viewpoint, especially when their vision forced many of them to dissent against public consensus. But for a time they were able to promote a public ethics, by example, fiat, instruction, and occasionally by law.

Conservative religionists, in many cases, were threatened or inconvenienced by this promotion. Some of them claimed that churches had no right to mingle politics with religion, that churches should have no public side. Others were put off by the fact that religious leaders chose to make equality the issue, when this ran against prejudice in the heart or equity in home investments. They found abhorrent and unpatriotic the effort by clerically collared demonstrators to protest a war about which they themselves were uneasy. But even more, these intransigents complained that religious demonstrators, as liberals, had changed the moral program. The faith had little to do with public virtue and the issues of justice, freedom, and equality. Those were merely political matters. The Christian standard had to do chiefly with virtue and vice that one could control in private life. Here liberals often looked like traitors.

Theologically, these liberals, by promoting critical views of the Bible, seemed to undercut the absolute standard on which conservatives based their views of private morality. By accepting scientific theories of human evolution they played into the hands of those who, for a century and more, had seen humans not in the image of God but merely as socially evolved beings ruled by a selfish gene and whatever standards they found currently attractive. In the debased world of bumper-stickers they fought a war over "the new morality," and a widely discussed but seldom understood "situation ethics." As the enemies of these, and some of their more glib defenders, had it, there were no principles or standards, no norms or guides except love. But love could easily give in to passions or be sentimentalized, when tests came.

In the 1970s, when these conservatives who had been left out in the sixties gained churchly power, they could point to a decline in private morality as projected into the public world. The crime rate grew, and crime, in their view, is after all the result of a delinquent individual's private choice and not a product of social circumstance. Television and popular media displayed forms of cohabitation or casual views of marriage that offended those who held to inherited views of monogamous, lifelong, marital bonding. Homosexuals came out of the closet and met new public acceptance, but these moralists saw homosexuality as a clear violation of stated and scriptured prohibitions. The movement for the liberation of women challenged their views of wifely submission, and the call for liberalization of abortion laws countered their view of the humanity of the foetus.

In the face of these changes, the "private" party of Christians, Protestant and Catholic alike, began to wear a public mask. These partisans had gained enough power and, through access to media and mailing devices, knew enough techniques to know how to produce a political effect. Some of them acknowledged that theirs was an about-face. Their inerrant Bibles had earlier told them inerrantly not to try to legislate morality. Now just as inerrantly they were told *to* legislate it, not because the Bible had changed but because immorality was so far-reaching that they had to alter their theology and outlook to meet the problem. The heirs of the liberal social theologians of a generation before were somewhat more passive. They had lost some power or had joined in a general retreat into the private world. The aggressiveness of the privatists by 1980 led many of the old-line public policy advocates in Christianity to complain that their churchly antagonists unfairly advocated "single issues."

This they did, but they clustered the issues into an alternative social program. Its philosophy was fairly coherent. First, hated views of scientific evolution had to go. Since it was impossible to conceive of most scientists as going, "going" came to mean balancing or challenging evolutionary teaching in the textbooks with "scientific creationism." A coterie of scientists was summoned to say that the biblical account of creation matched one reading of science. This, they said, should be taught in the schools, in order to break the monopoly that evolution held. Such challenging would lead to a loss of privilege among teachers of evolution and thus to a loss of faith in the theory. Soon again children would regain the biblical view of special creation and the divine image.

Children needed moral guidance by a sense of closeness to God. Next in the link of issues was talk of restoring prayer and Bible reading to the schools. In *Engel v. Vitale* and *Abington School District v. Schempp* in 1962 and 1963, the U.S. Supreme Court struck down efforts to impose or provide devotion and Bible reading in the schools. The schools were for education, not for devotion. They might and should teach about religion, but a pluralistic society should not set out through school devotions to inculcate religion. In the Court's eye, all religion was particular—even the gestures of meditation. In the eye of school prayer amendment advocates, the Bible was the book of the American founders and the American majority, and it should have a privileged place. Then people would have a code book from which to draw absolutes.

Most of the ensuing issues were congenial to the party of "private" Protestants, now joined by some Catholics, since they had less to do with elimination of poverty, an address to issues of racial inequality, or a reduction of the hazards of war. Instead, they had more to do with what issued from the bedroom and the closet. They linked up to oppose abortion and to seek a constitutional amendment to forbid it. They were against the Equal Rights Amendment since it did not teach womanly submission and might lead women out of the home, thus weakening the fundamental institution of the family. Vehemently they worked against homosexual rights legislation. They wanted legal limits on speech and the press through restrictions on materials that they found obscene or pornographic.

While some leaders recognized that to work for constitutional amendments and laws through lobbies and letters and ballots was a form of public and political activity, most of them succeeded in telling themselves that they were still essentially the private church concerned with private life. They were interested in piety and morality, not in politics, though they might have to support political candidates and parties to retain this private vision. Critics found it easy to deride them for their about-face and the rationale for it. It was also not hard to see why they fought to retain or win back a world they cherished, one that was fast slipping away from them. Nor was it hard to make fun of their causes, though it was impossible to lure one of them away through sarcasm and satire. Such instruments only proved to partisans that those who opposed them were of the devil or belonged to the conspiracy of secular humanists.

What became necessary was an understanding of their hurts. I have found it appropriate to think of this belligerent party along the lines of an ethnic group. Whereas the ethnic groups are all minorities—even WASPS of native WASP parentage make up less than thirty percent of the population—these moralists laid claim to majority sentiment on some causes and to priority and dominance based on the good old days of the American past. Since most of what they were doing was not illegal, there was no point in complaining that they violated American or Christian rules of the game. They had merely learned their own version of legislating morality after having despised it in others. For liberals to complain of their single-issue politics came with ill grace. Two or three generations earlier many of the liberals had made a single issue of prohibition: never vote for a legislator who is for repeal. Only one generation earlier many had made the war in Vietnam a single issue: never back anyone in politics who supports the war. Now it was difficult to be plausible by ruling out of the game those who said one should never support a politician who supported abortion.

Two other strategies were in place. The first was to begin the difficult but vaguely promising task of winning these partisans over to more complex views of the republic. In part, this was possible on theological grounds. Biblical literalists have to confront the texts, texts which give far more space to justice among classes of people or to the problem of poverty than to the issue of profanity or pornography. Yes, one must say to them, let us take the prophets literally, as you claim to. "It is written, and I insist . . ." is a phrase that would have great power. The potency of social passion among evangelicals, who take biblical authority strenuously and then try to effect biblical social visions in their story and through them in society, is a clue to the potential rewards of this strategy. Along with this theological reasoning comes a political argument. Those who oppose the political program would do well to empathize and to give recognition for those aspects of the private program that deserve commendation. Millions who hold to it are law abiding and they promote the public weal by not creating social problems. Many of them are generous in their private lives. Some of them address issues like poverty through inadequate but still symbolically and even practically valid commitments. Those fed by fundamentalists are not likely to have the political comprehension to take time to criticize them for not supporting welfare reform. But in addition to these mitigating factors, many of the people in the private church party after it became politically assertive, have not had occasion to see the implications of what they are doing for the whole republic. While it is not wise to underestimate their passion, it is also not judicious to underestimate their intelligence. The voting patterns of religious privatists are not predictable on all fronts. In the 1930s support for what others called socialism on a grand scale, the Tennessee Valley Authority, came also from populists whom others would have dismissed as fundamentalists, but who were voting for their self-interest.

Today it is in the self-interest of such populists to elect people to congress who will work for their economic good and their social security. To elect someone simply because he or she opposes the Equal Rights Amendment for women or supports a school prayer amendment may very well work to their long-term detriment if a candidate offers nothing else commendable.

The other grand half of a strategy is to counter with argument and power. Here the public church, if it undertakes considerable self-criticism and self-appraisal, can become an instrument in coalition with others to work for a different concept of the republic. This has even been a special calling of the public church. In recognizing this form of Christian organization and coalition, I am not saying, "Get together in order to have power," though all gettings-together have some sort of acquiring of power in view. Nor is this the point to say, "Organize over against others," though some ecumenical coalition has had the enemy in view. Instead, the call is to the participants in the public church individually and collectively to be faithful to the Christian, public, and common weal.

Mention public ethics to church people today and you are likely to meet elders who greet the call with a sense of *déjà vu,* and their offspring with furled brows of noncomprehension. The middle and senior generation are exhausted by recall of tensions within the churches from the last time they asserted themselves in the public realm in the era stamped "the sixties." One of the most promising aspects of the passing of a subsequent generation is that the 1960s need no longer dominate people in search of models for the public church. By the end of the 1980s, clearly half of the population will not be of a cohort that was born when John F. Kennedy became president, when he promoted the New Frontier, when Martin Luther King was in his prime with a dream of racial justice, or when Pope John XXIII called a council for reform and renewal. Lacking a living memory of the sixties, half of adult America itself will need to be told a story. They will be out from under the thrall of the negative features of that era, even if they live as beneficiaries of its positives. And there were many of these.

To move out of the shadow of the last round of public assertiveness means that the churches can reach into a repository of options and not be limited by their own reflexive memories. In the sixties there were or were perceived to be three stereotypical instruments available to denominational and ecumenical agencies or churchly causes. Most church people, we must remember, then as now were apathetic or benumbed. They cared about saved souls, personal health, the loyalty of the young across the generation gap, and Saturday night's party. They were benumbed by dissent and bemused by radical clerics. Most of them responded to poll-takers exactly as people of their location and class responded apart from Christian faith or life in the church. We are talking, then, about the ideas of elites, not majorities. But ideas have consequences and, for a moment, these elites produced effects of public consequence.

First of these forms was the denominational or ecumenical pronouncement. Easy to deride today, this form often had some effect. The churches then seemed more intact, and legislators had not yet learned how religous institutions had undergone a crisis of legitimacy comparable to the one secular institutions were experiencing. The lawmakers and public had not yet been able to demythologize the pronouncement-making process. Incredible as it seems today, ethicists like Paul Ramsey and Paul Harrison, at the height of pronouncement making, felt it necessary to ask *Who Speaks for the Churches?* They made news by showing that most pronouncements reflected the views of unrepresentative elites in bureaucratically organized churches. Such analysts as critics did not fault task forces for talking *to* the churches. They simply decried the illusion that these spoke *for* the consensus and power of the churches or that their views were necessarily the only ones appropriate to those churches. A generation later the public is wise to the limits of the bureaucratic or conventional (which means gathered-in-convention) church institution. Where it is not, the legislator is. To hear that the Board of Social Concern of the United Methodist Church in the name of twelve-million Methodists demands that the Congress do something about an issue like housing or amnesty has no effect on a Methodist congressperson who has antennae out and who never meets a Methodist who makes such demands—or who would not oppose them.

In the retrospect of a generation there is no reason to make fun of the process and the pronouncement. In one catalytic moment, they spoke a truth and they spoke it with power. At their best, these pronouncements resulted from processes that reached into or, even better, grew from, study in the congregations or cells of a church body. Where that was a romantic picture, they still derived from deliberations by representative bodies or by responsible leaders like bishops, who stand in some sort of political relations to congregants. Again at their best, they reached into the deeper traditions of a Christian movement and used these to judge or inspire people captive of more recent and less lively pasts. The potential for pronouncements remains. When the Southern Baptist Convention through its ambassadors in convention voted 20,000 to 0 for reduction in arms in the very year when America turned more armament conscious, the rest of America had to pay some attention to an awakening among the largest Protestant body. Or the Baptists have to live with their elegant act of mistiming, since a few months later hawkish zeal was back in fashion. The convention resolution or bureaucratic pronouncement, however, simply is not an instrument to spook out opponents or to rally the troops, if it ever was.

Second is the demonstration. To demonstrate is to show forth. It takes no great act of translation to discover the biblical roots of such activity. To accompany the words of the mouth with the placement of a body is a gesture or witness of intrinsic value in certain circumstances. To place one's self in physical jeopardy as a Protestant minister in Protestant Selma or in the garb of a nun in Catholic Cicero, Illinois, momentarily was a sign of courage more than of folly. To risk imprisonment by a law that many regarded as unjust in the name of a higher law may not always have won much more than grudging admiration, but it had telling effect. To amass thousands of people in support of a cause made a point that was not visible in editorials or the mails. To inconvenience one's self and one's community until it takes action or until outside action comes was a form of witness that in Christian context carried a special weight. In the era of mass communications, of course, it was easy to exploit the demonstration since the camera followed action not in the classroom but in the schoolyard, not in the committee room but in the streets.

So long as demonstration grew out of the commitment of people who surprised others with their presence, it had an effective charm. So long as people were able therewith to clarify their vision of a better society and not merely to protest the present one, they found followers. And so long as the demonstrators exemplified a sacrificial way of life, they had to call forth response. But soon Christian demonstration became confused. Some still say *agents provocateurs* of the government, along with unrooted and anomic radical forces, joined the ranks. Demonstrations began to lose power. As soon as they became predictable or when the public caught on to the media fascination with action of any sort, the demonstration began to lose its power. Today it is not necessarily without effect, but the odds are against it producing much beside yawns or counter-effects. The day may come when it will again be effective in more circumstances. For now, the ghost of the sixties is gone, and so is its effective tactic.

The third instrument was the persistent activity of the church as a political agency, or as political agencies of the churches. In many metropolitan areas there were "industrial missions" which worked to bring the faith into the market, the corporation, or urban planning. Most members of the churches were never aware of this form of think tank or action pool. Many denominations kept representatives in Washington to speak up for the causes. Two problems afflicted such agencies. First, they were often a product of mere bureaucratization. In the midst of the era of religious social action, Henry Pratt wrote a scholarly analysis of *The Liberalization of American Protestantism.* The book was mistitled. Nowhere did it deal with classic themes of liberalism in Christianity: the close relation of nature and supernature, transcendence and immanence, Christian and humane culture. Instead, it chronicled the rise of the National Council of Churches as an expression of Max Weber's *Rationalität,* a gear-meshing, often impersonal force. The bureaucrats were not necessarily people of ill will. Many expressed Christian faith and creativity. But they were also agents and products of modern processes that almost by definition kept them from a close tie with the people who made up the rest of the churches.

The second problem that blighted this form and makes it less effective in the public church today had to do with the kind of power then asserted. Many were critical then and more are now of the tendency that conceives of the church merely or largely as a political agency. Today the temptation is smaller because the perception of power has decreased. But some bureaucratic leaders acted as if churchly participation was inescapable, just as life in political society is. If citizens do not want to be part of political society, they have no place to hide. If they migrate or go into exile, they become a part of the new home place. The state can reach them with coercive forms of law, taxation, licensing, and draft registration.

Conceiving of the church in such terms is a disastrous carry-over of establishmentarian thought from earlier centuries. Once upon a time there was "no salvation outside the church," which meant outside the visible and dominant church. Excommunication ruled victims out of sacramental life and thus probably out of heaven beyond. The interdict against a Catholic regime hampered the path to salvation of a Catholic population. Most churches in a free society do not have such coercive power. If the Southern Presbyterians became too courageous in matters of racial policy, they could not coerce continued support or membership. Their intransigent members could shift to the Southern Baptists, who as they grew increasingly courageous drove people to Churches of Christ. Some of their units got the spirit and left people free to find a final home in the Independent Fundamental church-of-their-choice.

Since the churches are escapable, and each individual church is easily so, and since they cannot tax, raise armies, or coerce, the only powers they have are the powers of shared belief, uniting prayer, common memory, fusing hope, impelling mutual love. One cannot long live off the inherited capital of previous generations. The interest will not last. Someone has to invest new spiritual energies. Some leaders in the 1960s knew that Dorothy Day and Martin Luther King and their kind were profound Catholics or Baptists who fed and were fed on scripture, prayer, and common worship. But not all their counterparts understood this and were rewarded by foot dragging on the part of coparticipants who did not share their reading of a social program and were ignored by the larger society.

The point here is not a purely pragmatic one. It is not sufficient to say that these forms do not work, and therefore they should be abandoned. If they are appropriate, one makes them work. Nor is this all only a vision born of hindsight, as if to say, "if only we had known then what we know now, we would not have been active." Maybe Americans should be glad they did not know then what they know now, or the benefits of the former actions would not be with us. More likely, Christians did know then what we know now, but they recognized a *kairos*, an especially urgent and pregnant instant, and acted in spite of realism. Certainly, believers should not work on the assumption that elements of the church dare speak only when everyone in them agrees, for then they should never speak. The point instead is that the form of a full generation ago, the one that shadows and blights the public church today, is not the eternal, only, and inclusive policy. A later generation can make selective use of it, but relativizes it and thus frees the imagination.

To that end, a verbal slide show of a few images of past forms can serve as antecedents to the public church's more recent pattern of pronouncing, demonstrating, and politically acting. Instead of detailing, I shall only call forth certain historical images in order to increase the possibility of producing a relativizing and, in this case, freeing effect.

In the first generation, Bartolomeo de Las Casas, who some believe was the first Christian ordained in the New World, was a holder of Indian slaves. One day he read a scripture in Ecclesiasticus and was called to preach on it. The text pronounced a woe on those who lived unjustly off the labors of others. Las Casas thereupon began a reversal that, alas, did not soon enough exclude blacks, but he did speak up for Indian rights. The priest played off interest against interest back in Spain; he challenged slaveholders in his bishopric at risk to his own life and spent decades as the sorrowing friend of the Indians. Las Casas and his often scorned fellow missioners in Catholic New Spain in many cases moderated or checked the *conquistadores* and consistently worked toward more humane relations.

Then, in the first Protestant generation, Puritans read biblical texts that pictured a commonwealth of order and justice with its own kind of freedoms. They conceived of themselves as a people chosen to complete church reformation and envisioned a society that in many, too many details, was to embody the theocracy of Moses as they learned of him in their Old Testaments. Far from being *laissez faire* economists, as later free market people would see these foreparents of early America, they planned every aspect of economic life from the just price to regulation of interest. Later generations may not find congruence between their own ideals of justice for the whole society and the Puritan ideals, but few informed people would find the foreparents lacking in an imagination of the church public.

The Anabaptist and Quaker dissenters, soon after, did not accept the Puritan imposition and worked to separate civil and religious realms. But this did not mean that they were interested only in private salvation. Many of the Baptists took strong stands with the patriots because they believed that they must extend political freedom as they had supported ecclesiastical freedom. The Quakers under

William Penn in his sylvania tried to effect a holy commonwealth of voluntary assent to the spirit's norms.

Image four: New Amsterdam citizens began to teach and live with pluralism, though its governors like Peter Stuyvesant were repressive types. If they could not come up with a polity to legitimate the presence of Jews, Catholics, Lutherans, and other misfits, they devised a policy of "conniving" to make the society work, for commercial benefit and Christian concord.

Many of the current embodiments of the revivalist tradition make up the private party in the church, and do so in the name of their pioneers. This is a mistaken reading. Certainly, the people of Jonathan Edwards's and George Whitefield's day in the 1740s, of the Wesleyans in the 1780s, or the revivalists of the 1800s were God-intoxicated and apparently single-issue people when it came to preaching release for the soul along with conversion. It would be a misreading to turn them into fundamentally political thinkers even if they produced political effects. But after conversion they did not simply ask people to keep producing Born Again autobiographies. They were called to "spread scriptural holiness throughout the land." They worked for moral renovation through a pattern of benevolent and reform agencies and sometimes through legislation. All this produced a sixth image: a millennial wing that worked overtly to shape a better society in the image and hope of the Peaceable Kingdom or the Second Coming.

Freedmen's bureaus by and for blacks were welfare agencies. In their militant forms, they linked up with abolitionists or were abolitionist. Thus they tore at the fabric of southern and, indirectly, all of American society in the most rending of all crises of our history.

More pluralist images: Jews came in such numbers in the 1880s that they put some of their formerly religious energies not into synagogues but social service agencies. Many of these looked secular, but down to our own time Jewish scholars have shown how, even in the case of the militantly secular versions, these laborite or socialist causes invoked the prophets themselves against Judaism and employed consciences formed by the Torah to work for their interests and for justice against those encrusted in the synagogue or against non-Jews.

In the 1890s a young seminarian named John Ryan, tutored by a congenial archdiocese under an encouraging Archbishop John Ireland at Saint Paul, read papal documents of Leo XIII. These supported social justice, and so did the young new convert to Leonine views. Ryan and colleagues for decades, well past the New Deal, worked for minimum wages, rights of labor, and a just society. Here is a tenth example of Americans who did not wait for the model of the activists of the sixties. For an eleventh, too obvious to require elaboration, was the meliorist and nonviolent but still radical envisioning and working for the Kingdom of God by the agents of the Social Gospel. Or, twelve, the social criticism of the Niebuhr era, which was a radical criticism of its parent Social Gospel. Except during a brief Marxian stage, the Niebuhrian social realists were not utopian. They made use of grimly realistic checks on idealism but never lost their passion for justice. Concurrent with the social activists in Catholicism and mainline Protestantism, a cohort of "young evangelicals" of all ages proved that one need not be politically liberal to use biblical norms against injustice.

Between the gaps of these thirteen brief images, or attached as variations to them, are scores of models that antedate, complement, and sometimes contradict but always qualify the monopoly of sixties-style ethical involvements. And many features of those last styles survive. Though church growth experts sometimes suggested that mainline churches declined because of their engagements in the sixties, careful surveys suggest that there were few losses or even few withholdings of financial support over the social commitment. Those who opposed the mainline approach on other terms could hitchhike on discontents over social activity to disengage themselves to take others into schism. But the sixties phase died more of exhaustion than over protest; the world and church moved on.

We seem now to be back at base one. In the reconstruction at base one many in the public church are rediscovering some insights cherished in the private Christian parties. One is that shared belief and prayer continue to have their potency. Another is that it does make a difference how individual participants order their outlook and ethics. A pioneer in spreading this insight is Stanley Hauerwas, a stray Southern Methodist in snowbelted Notre Dame, who speaks of an ethics of character. With Aristotle he asks how the person comes to be good in the sense that he or she characteristically does good things toward good ends. And he draws on the story of Jesus to ask what is Christianly distinctive about a good character and how does it get formed. In a complex world a person in ethical straits, for example, a physician in a medical moral dilemma, cannot convoke an ecumenical council or an ethical task force. He or she has to have a good character formed by access to principles, revelation, and a supportive community.

Base one leads to base two. A society is not an aggregate of individuals of good character any more than the public church is an agglomeration of atomized individuals. Society and church are made up of components, *symbiotes*, interests that live with and off one another. This means that on the agenda for the public church is the call to contribute to social and public morale. Morale is a hard-to-define term, but it connotes an aspect of spirit that animates morals and mores. Many social critics, economist Robert Heilbroner among them, have in recent years noted that individuals in society are concerned with private morale without seeing its context. In late stages of a business civilization, they line up for their Master of Business Administration degrees and the goodly material benefits of commerce and the professions, without devoting themselves to rationalizing the reality off which they live. And that reality is not likely to survive assaults in the face of economic breakdowns.

The public church, concerned as it is with the spiritual side of private morale, is especially called to stimulate public and social morale. External crises help, as they did in the Second World War. Concern for ending the Nazi-fascist threat and the survival of a common civilization inspired public morale. Any visitor to Israel can see how common threats help displace the factionalisms and private interests, however precariously. Demagogues anywhere may conjure up a single external threat until it papers over internal differences. But most Americans are likely to have to live with pluralism among themselves and with a plurality of challenges, none of which is likely to generate social morale unless there be generators. The public church is only one among the instruments for stimulating such morale, as its contribution to the human republic.

On base one of an ethic of character and on the fundament of public morale, there is, third, an awakening of local expressions toward a public ethic. Public church participants are not adept at the use of mass media for rallying support, in part because their message depends on subtleties that media like television do not allow for. They are in reaction against the remoteness and impersonality of their own bureaucracies, sometimes to the point that they overlook their gifts. They share some of the antifederalist populism that is widespread in a political order that wanly looks for reformulation. It is clear that in the immediate future in a free society many people are going to choose participation in religious life as a means of fighting back against *Rationalität* and administration-from-afar. They will seek to use more immediate and malleable forms, and the local congregation stands the chance of being one of these.

Critics say that the self-interest of churches at Youngstown, Ohio, was responsible for a new ecumenical expression, but it was significant that the ecumenical coalition was among the more assertive agencies when a crisis came to the city after the closing of the steel mills. There was no sudden national awakening to the nuclear jeopardy, but the churches in the locale of Three-Mile Island in Pennsylvania quickly found or developed experts and expertise on the subject. When mass communicators ask to see grand new movements for social activism in the churches, the people they ask can be impressively numb and dumb. But if we can take such communicators on what one might call an "infrared camera" tour of the warmth-lines of many urban areas, they will see all kinds of local attempts to contribute to the public order.

The tour would begin with black churches, which have not lost their voice for eternity or their tie to politics, good and somtimes bad. Or there would be stops at those nexuses of churches which contribute to welfare. And there would be camera angles on countless local churches or connections between them to meet the needs of migrant workers, the aged, people on drugs, or in need of food or housing.

Some radical critics would say that these ameliorating agencies distract from the revolution we need; one that would bring down multinational corporations, institutionalized injustice, or unimaginative ecclesiasticism. Certainly, these glimpses do not represent high drama. But they are the first child steps after paralysis set in a half generation ago. They have intrinsic value, are instrumentally good for the people they connect, and can be parables of directions the society and church may take. From those tentative steps people can regain confidence.

The public church in its constituencies, including the local, has the means for overcoming romantic rejections of technology and employing technological means to address problems. A generation ago the poets of the counterculture acted as if one could enter a commune, find a ravine, and strum a guitar or sitar while chanting *om*, to make pollution go away. But those poets lacked staying power or integrity. They made their witness against capitalism off dad's pocket and against technology using electronic amplifiers—and the problems outlasted them. The question is not: is a technological order avoidable? It will not be. Even a demodernizing Iran wants the hardware of technology, though interpreted in different ways. Over the long pull populations *are* going to choose its mixed benefits. The issue is: is a *humane* technological order possible?

The public church says that the technological possibility occurs inside the scope of the Lord of history. Its many components and constituents will not agree on a specific way of employing this possibility toward humane order. The public church does not exist to produce homogeneity. It calls upon all interests and sides within it to subject their vision to the word of God and the message of the churches. There is no danger of running out of issues thus to be subjected. So long as much of the world is dependent upon non-renewable sources of energy, the debates over access to them and priorities for development of renewable ones will tear the society apart. Dependencies of this sort will assure inflation and other threats to the economy and force international contesting and other threats to peace. A corollary to these economic and energy issues has to do with environment. If the churches of the sixties called the civil rights struggle and a localized war a crisis and a *kairos,* they must find words to express another crisis and urgency: within the next two generations fateful and permanent choices having to do with ozone and ocean will have been made. These choices include technological addresses and theological understandings. Romantics who seek demonstrations and radical action are slowly learning the difference between issues of the sixties and eighties. Now it is not "integrate or disintegrate," "stay in or get out." Now to agitate for one use of energy calls forth a different form of pollution. To see the need for development by using one kind of pesticide issues in possibilities of cancer, and to see a reason to use none promotes certain starvation.

Theological issues are manifest. The whole public church owns a scripture that on page one points to creator and creation, to stewardship that does not mean thoughtless dominion by humans. Most of the public church sees creation in line one of its creeds and custodianship of earth throughout its affirmations. The first chapters of any number of New Testament books include the language of "all." All things, the whole creation, are linked to the redemption of the children of God. Later chapters spell out life in the New Creation, foretasted now.

Countering these theological commitments are others that come at the end of the Bible or the creed and that can easily be pulled out of context until they dominate. There are good and certain reasons to fear the years between now and 2000. If the year 1000 is any guide, one has to reckon with the human propensity toward numerology and superstition about calendar accidents. For no rational or biblically prophesied reasons the end of a millennium will inspire even more millennial specifying than it already has. Certainly, there are enough signs of the times, there always have been, to legitimate urgency. Armageddon in a literal sense needs no dispensationalist prophet. One can look at the daily newspaper and without guidance expect such a dénouement to world history. But there are special reasons now for prophets to hang out shingles or peddle books linking page one with biblical last chapters. The effort appeals to *gnosis,* to knowing more about the end of time than Jesus himself professed to know. It is a satisfying act to give up on *The Late Great Planet Earth* before God does. To believe that one cannot reformulate society, licenses only the rescue of souls along with hedonism, both spiritual and sunny-beached. The public church, however, without forgetting the note of urgency, does not simply shape a gnostic elite for the end-time but is especially called to project that language of the end two billion years ahead and ask how the next generation makes the world, under God, one in which care and 'responsibility survive and matter.

The public church is not so likely to be afflicted by literal premillennialism toward 2000 as by a tendency toward private invention and the celebration of introverted religious signals. The widely advocated therapies and celebrations find a special appeal among those who have only private instincts in the public church. "Have you had the experience?" "Our encounter group really put me in touch with myself." Something of the Aquarian hope lives on. Economist and good-natured mystic Kenneth Boulding brought people up short when the hippies of yore advocated the Aquarian age. Boulding noted that Aquarius was the only zodiacal character who was doing any work. He trudged eternally across the heavens with his water pots, thus embodying the Presbyterian work ethic. What the twenty-first century will need, Boulding added, is Aquarian hard work. Mysticism is integral to spiritual life, and prayer is vital to the Christian version. But there also has to be attention to development. People have to eat. In Peguy's terms: "Everything begins in mysticism and ends in politics."

Stewardship of the earth, attentiveness to the issues of poverty and hunger and inequality, development or the liberation of peoples or both, war and peace: I leave to others the stimulant to imagination to make those issues live and would debase them by dull and cursory notice of each. *How* the public church addresses issues is the present concern, and I can illustrate that better with attention to somewhat more domestic issues, for which expertise already exists in most congregations or larger constituencies. These include ethics of the professions and concern for medical, legal, and similar delivery and decision.

For years our pragmatic and pluralist society coasted along with its suggestion that it could settle all issues of law, medicine, or business by the traditions of the professions, by legal history and the good sense of physicians or traders. As issues became more complex, some despaired of *any* civil conversation and retreated into private worlds. Then as scandals unfolded in the administration of justice, controversy arose in the understanding of the medical dimensions of the life cycle, and corruption apeared in the world of business—to mention only three professions that have almost all citizens in their clienteles—there grew new interest in seeing the ethical issues within the field of public discourse. For that, as Father John Courtney Murray once observed, it became necessary to "go up higher" into some level of ethics, metaphysics, or theology.

In the case of law, the object or end is to resolve the problem of securing the social order. This it does by regulating social institutions, adjudicating claims between contenders among them, and the like. In some respects it must give support to standards of society and make possible transactions between people in it. This is familiar in the language of legal intention. What results is a kind of regard for law as a "meta-institution," with superintending functions. Philip Hammond has shown that in order to carry out its functions, the law took on the character of the civil religion in America. One can easily draw analogies between it and the sacral aspects of medicine, and it does not take much seeking to find ways in which Americans see the professions of business supporting a quasi-religious market system.

Where, however, does one find the language for "going up higher" into ethics, communicating in the sphere of superintending "meta-institutions," or, worst of all, providing discourse in theology?

One set of contenders argues at once that it is possible to overcome pluralism and to be ever in the processof doing so. Three spheres for this come to mind. One is a synthesis provided by world civilization. A law of reason must operate on such broad and general terms that the separate religions and tribalisms must give way to it. Philosopher of history Erich Kahler spoke of the need and hunger that provided an appeal for such synthesis: "Everything is in flux, everything is open to questin, everything is involved in perpetual change and dissolution." As religion lost its hold on publics or as freedom spread choice and diversity between and within the faiths, what William Barrett called religion's function as a "psychic container" dissolved. Populations had a sense of "homelessness." Yet people dreamed of integration around a single spiritual synthesis. Philosopher William E. Hocking had spoken of three ways toward that end: "radical displacement," in which one religious outlook would prevail; "the way of synthesis," which would draw in the several world views and faiths, and "the way of reconception," which looked toward revision of faith and metaphysics or meta-institutions.

As widely propagated as those visions were at mid-century, they have all but vanished today. In dusty, crabbed corners of World Integration societies, too small to support their postage, or in Vanity Press books, which only friends of authors receive and only parents endure to read, this cosmic vision lives under eclipse. What happened? One could say that visionaries too readily succumbed to the massive and convulsive ingatherings of people into tribes, too quickly fed into the appeal for separate identities. But there were more practical and noble reasons. Anthropologists despaired of finding universals and their work promoted cultural relativism or mere agnosticism. The examples of demodernizing synthesis and the overcoming of variety and choice came effectively only through costly coercive systems like Maoism. For the short pull—a century? a millennium?— Thomas Mann's dictum looked like the prospect: the world has many centers and it is not likely to find integration. As Warren Wagar also asked, "Who will integrate the integrators?"

However valuable world synthesis or integration may be, practically there could be an address to the ethical issue if, within one society as complex and problematic as America's, there could be more interaction. As a result, one hears some prophecies that Americans will weary of pluralism and seek a single coercive civil religion through the deification of the state and the assignment to it of the right to do all norm setting. Robert Heilbroner, a socialist economic historian who is not at all happy with business civilization in decline, thinks that the public is also unhappy with that civilization as it disintegrates. No longer does it provide moraleor carry a rationale for enough of the public to sustain itself through a drastic crisis. Inflation is endemic to such a society, and there are limits to the growth on which it depends. An economic crash could lead to massive reorganization on some sort of socialist scale that Heilbroner does not find wholly uncongenial. While he cherishes individual liberties, critical intelligence, and untrammeled scientific exploration, Heilbroner expects that he and others will have to learn to live with less than utopian curtailing of these virtues. So badly will citizens need a rationale for the adjustments they must make as they find pluralism distracting that they will assent to state deification. Then the symbols of the civil religion would provide a skein of commonality for "going up higher." Heilbroner does not spell out the content of the new synthesis. I would have to draw on the two heritages of Christianity and Enlightenment, however corrupted these may be since the last social contract was written late in the eighteenth century. To seal itself and provide reassurance, then, it would probably be called Christian Democracy.

At this stage, however, hungry though they may be for some aspects of synthesis—witness the people who want *their* absolutes to govern all, or *their* revealed religion to set the norms for everyone—when it is spelled out, most citizens find the coercive element unattractive. Then a more informal form of civil or public religion propagates itself. This faith distils from the witness of the churches, the republican tradition, and various philosophies, a view of transcendent justice. Such a norm, it is said, informed the Declaration of Independence and the Constitution, the theology of Abraham Lincoln during the deepest national crisis, the Kennedy inaugural address, and the first announcements of the Johnson Great Society.

As with world synthesis, so with civil religion; advocates had to ask what to do with existing varieties of faith. Some drew on John Dewey's *A Common Faith,* written in the 1930s. Dewey was for religion but not for theism, for social process but not for social institutions like the church. He supported faith not in God but in democracy, and he spoke for "radical displacement," to use Hocking's term. The last line of his book called for the civil religion to become explicit and militant. J. Paul Williams in the 1950s refined the call by asking that democracy be taught as the very will of God. Williams wanted it supported by metaphysical sanction and ceremonial reinforcement.

Somewhat more moderate was Sidney E. Mead, religious historian and philosopher of the public realm who advocated a "religion of the republic" that strikes me as being a synthesis, though with Enlightenment ideology entrenched in the privileged position. Some days Mead sounded militant against the pluralism of the distracting sects, but more often he was merely explicit and asked that the sects be exposed as irrelevant to the public weal. Leave them alone and they'll go home, to tend to private hungers for salvation that have nothing to do with public order. Several years after, at the twilight moment of the Kennedy-Johnson (or King-Roncalli) collapse of dreams, Robert N. Bellah gave eloquent voice to a civil religion that followed the pattern of "reconception." He was less eager than Dewey to see church religion as a rival or than Mead to see it as irrelevant. But Bellah, while sending churches a card of thanks for feeding faith and symbolization into the civil religion, and later regretting that the churches could not do more restoring after "the broken covenant" became apparent, believed that the main energies should go into the common zone of religious symbols.

One can see how through the nineteenth and twentieth centuries the United States Supreme Court tried to cope with this civil religion at the base of law. In the 1890s one still heard the language of a Christian nation. In the 1950s a dictum in *Zorach v. Clauson,* still curiously quoted in the 1960s, held that "we are a religious people," a certifiable proposition, followed by the less warrantable claim that "our institutions presuppose a Supreme Being." Philosopher Sidney

Hook took the court to task for that possibly reflexive quotation and later self-quotation. Many, if not all, of the founders believed in a Supreme Being, but they took pains not to prescribe that faith in their charter documents or to penalize any who did not hold it. Supreme Beings evidently got along for millennia without the American kind of institutions. And republican institutions are logically and practically possible and supported by people who do not include a Supreme Being in their presuppositions. Why, while quoting it then, did the court weaken faith in such a Supreme Being by ruling out devotion or prayer directed to it in public forums?

Later in the 1960s, in two often overlooked conscientious objection cases, *Seeger* and then *Welch*, the Court had to broaden its concept of synthesis or reconception. In one case, the Court justices admitted that one could be religious in the world, and hence in America, without recourse to a Supreme Being. In the second, it went on to say that one could be conscientious enough to object to military service without the support or solace of anything so formal as religion. But the objector could arrive at his position by humanistic and social scientific routes which, without saying so, the Court was urging be regarded as sacral. By now the civil religion was becoming so diffuse that it was ungraspable. It hardly provided a stable plateau, but only a jagged *arête*, for precarious climbers who would "go up higher," only to have to fall back to their separatenesses again.

Over against those three broad forums, two advocacies were designed to lead to a reconceived pluralism. John Courtney Murray gave voice to both and in some ways supported both. In his priorities, he would have a Thomist concept of natural law, a match for Walter Lippmann's public philosophy, but he wrote in a time when both were themselves falling into eclipse. Still, Murray did not want to see the notion of a *consensus juris*, an "agreement about fundamental values," fall into disuse and total decay. His own career showed something of the possibility for eloquent support of its benefits, and his philosophy has never died out. But this consensus, which was operating in the simpler Christian-enlightened elites of 1789, was less available and more qualified in latter-day pluralism. Who, one asks, provided the consensus by which to measure or even locate modern consensus?

Historian Daniel J. Boorstin once demonstrated or argued that America did not need content for its consensus so much as the process of debating it, the notion that one would be available. In a stunning image he compared the American arcanum or shrine to the Holy of Holies in the Jewish Temple in Jerusalem. The Romans had wanted to know what was in it, what was the locus of the holy and thus the motor behind the stamina and zeal of the pesty Jews. Therefore, said Heinrich Graetz, historian of the Jews, Pompey and his men eagerly stormed the Temple and broke in to the shrine to find only *that it was empty.* Americans similarly believed they had a creed but could not point to it or spell it out, they only kept a sacred space for it. When they *could* find it, they were not able to show how one came to confess it. If their creed was in the Declaration of Independence, that was not an official document to which school children or immigrants must subscribe. They only have to support the Constitution, not a notably creedal or metaphysical document.

Murray's other elaboration on the way to reconceive pluralism was a conspiracy theory. Conspirators "breathe together." So, he wrote, there were conspirators within at least four large population cohorts: Protestantism, Catholicism, Judaism, and a religiously perceived secular humanism. They were often at each others' throats when they should have been conspiring in search and support of consensus. At times Murray pictured them with different rationales for the same *consensus juris.* They looked like the components Benjamin Franklin coped with when he prescribed a "public religion," which was born of the intersections of philosophies and churches at the place where these had something in common.

A rereading of Murray places the positive possibilities of this view fairly near our concept of the *communitas communitatum* as formulated by Johannes Althusius. This federalist concept allows for decentralizing and yet for common effort. The *symbiotes* associate with one another, on different levels. So the interaction among churches, political parties, professions, and the like, demand and permit various levels of intimacy. The more levels, the more protection one has against Leviathan. And yet through interaction there is also a chance to develop common language. The most natural association for Althusius, though it is irrelevant in the present context, was that of kin and in families as clans, which were more or less convenanted.

The second scale was the *collegium,* which could be a profession, a professional association, a college or university, a guild, a circle for mutual aid, or anything which unites people toward definable purposes. Althusius even specified collegia for theologians and philosophers and for "magistrates and judges, and of various craftsmen, merchants, and rural folk." In the present analogy, these components lie within the public church and link it with others within the city. For Althusius the next level of association was the city, "the public association," which "exists when many private associations are linked together for the purpose of establishing an inclusive political order. It can be called a community, an associated body, or the preeminent political association." As noted earlier, Althusius lived in a late-medieval world, and his concept of city matches the larger commonwealth. The state or commonwealth is the inclusive political organization, but not one that ever becomes free to overlook the interests of all lower levels of association which make it up and provide checks against its power. The Calvinists themselves yielded authority to it only when something could not be settled on lower levels of specific association. In this respect he worked against many enlightened statist thinkers. "It is necessary . . . that doctrine of the symbiotic life of families, kinship associations, collegia, cities, and provinces precede the doctrine of the realm or universal symbiotic association that arises from the former associations and is composed of them."

Conservatives can easily commandeer this associational concept along with most other pluralisms. Pluralism, as Robert Nisbet has pointed out, relies on tradition, and the revolutionary seeks to overthrow that. There is room in it for localism, congregational or guild orientation, family and neighborhood. Leviathan, however, wants to do away with their power. The implied layering of associations amounts to a kind of hierarchy, which can easily be misread into something antiegalitarian. By allowing for autonomy and decentralizing, it is harder for the liberator by one stroke to liberate everything. But these conservative connotations are not the only way to read the symbiotic view of social and political life.

Instead, it has a place in what we might think of as a "two-button-to-push" relation. The public church and pluralist society live between two tendencies. On one hand, privatism and tribalism break down the possibility of public discourse. People are so sure of their identities that they trust no one outside their group. Over against them one stresses the "*community* of communities." This button is the one to be pressed in a time like our own when sectarianism and private morale disrupt even a basic concern for common discourse, when tribes are solipsistic and self-centered. But whenever and wherever a plural society wearies of its pluralism and is ready for the single savior or synthesis, the *symbiotes* can press the other button and accent the ways in which they are a "community of *communities.*"

Alongside efforts to overcome pluralism with universal norms or to reconceive pluralism, there is a cluster of calls for unreconstructed pluralism, for living with its discontents. The late articulator of humanist values Charles Frankel spelled out this version: "Social integration in a liberal society does not come from integrating ultimate values. It comes from organizing secular institutions in such a way that men's 'ultimate' values—their conscience, their sense of the meaning of life, their personal dignity—do not become elements of public conflict." A practical pluralism results; people despair of "going up higher" into theoretical realms and settle on making the process work. The process comes close to being the ultimate value.

America muddles through fairly well with this third approach. At certain moments, at least, what we may call tribal confederation has been effective. In Revolutionary War times, sectarian Baptists who despised the theology of infidel enlightened founders linked up with these founders, who themselves despised Baptist superstition and sectarianism. The result was a polity that produced religious freedom. But beyond tribal confederation are mere tribalism or individualism and the breakdown of the polis. All society can do in face of them is to coast or to evade the troubling issues.

The public church allows for all these alternatives in its address to the larger society, but in the present model something of the conspiracy approach inside public religion is most congenial. This stands against simple individualisms, in which all do what they please and where "everything is permitted." Whenever good occurs, this means only that the current whims of the majority in the society are satisfied. There are then no principles or hypotheses by which people live. The *symbiotic* view further opposed simple isolation of subcommunity life. Pascal: "How agreeable it is to determine justice by a river boundary. Truth is on this side of the Pyrenees, error on the other side." But their approach is not agreeable in a society where rivers and mountains do not provide the boundaries. The associational outlook stands over against insensitivity to subcommunity positions. It pays respect to the rootage of ideals with which it does not agree.

To the purists who seek absolutes, and some will also exist within the sphere of the public church, such an approach cannot be satisfying. It will seem to grant too much to cultural relativism or to the tribes. Philosopher Harry K. Girvetz spoke for them: "The mores can make anything right." But most participants have had to learn to settle for less neatness and more freedom in pluralism. They know that one can give a dog a bad name and by calling this one relativ*ism*, suggest more smelly confusion than there is. In most ethical choice there are not infinite options but one or two, grounded in coherent systems. In principle, the *creencias* of a society may be limitless. These *creencias* are, in Ortega's definition, the ideas that are so deep that one is hardly conscious of holding them. They are the ideas that one *is*, not the ideas that one *has*. For a recent illustration: the courts have been torn over the question whether society must notice race and compensate for past injustices in allocating opportunities and resources in society. To overlook race is to keep minorities at a disadvantage. To accent race is to live with outlooks that produced the problem. Good people may differ on the outcome, and the outcome has important consequences for policy. But what was significant and merited notice was this: no longer at issue were the society's *creencias;* they now called for some sort of concern for equality. The debaters were not at sea in relativism. They argued policy in a rather clarified concept.

Dredged from some probably obsolete anthropological argument are some lines of R. E. Money-Kyrle that bear translation. The bases of morality in this kind of society are neither a priori and universal, as the metaphysicians claimed, nor empirical and relative as critical philosophers maintained. Instead they are empirical *and* universal in the sense that they make up together a quality, like binocular vision or an articulated thumb, which is found to be common to all mankind. The anthropologist always comes up with a tribe whose practices limit the vision of a common human experience. Well and good, one must say, but that fact does not rule out the provisional bases for moral debate. In Clyde Kluckhohn's language, which has to be unsatisfying to totalists and tribalists, this kind of society lives by "conditional absolutes." Thus we may also think of Jefferson and the founders providing a working hypothesis for a possibly great society. The Hippocratic Oath and various professional codes do the same for various *collegia* within our society. Their understanding provides for better disagreement and less confusion than the mere competitive asserting of absolutes on bumper-stickers or settling for mere relativism and no possibility of "going up higher."

To demonstrate what some conditional absolutes are in the medical field, the "life and death" arena, let me set forth a few. Life is better than death. This is a conditional absolute for most people, who believe that one may well give a life for another. Others may find the life of a human reduced to vegetable status and can entertain that its pointlessness may legitimate a stop in the flow of artificial medical support—and thus death. But in both cases, those who argue know that they have to do so in the context of a value sacred to life. In medicine, even in a society that lives by law, one would get nearly universal support for the notion that the person is more important than the rule. The Sabbath was made for people, not people for the Sabbath. A third: duration of life is not the *only* value; there are also questions of the meaning and quality of life. Again: ethical decision is best made in the context of community. The patient belongs in theory, and usually in practice, to a family or circle of care, and lives in a society with traditions and norms. Decisions affecting persons have to connect them with that context. Common people, not only philosophers and ethicists, have opinions on these subjects and have given thought to them. The citizenry is not simply at sea.

Most of them would say, though not necessarily in these terms, that something in "philosophically principled" ethics is worth preserving. Principle allows for one to anticipate difficult and sudden decisions, so that one is not caught off guard. Through it people can make systematic sense of reality and thus retain trust. Each complex decision does not come point-blank at an unready public. So long as there is principle, there can be revising of it by people who know they *are* revising. Therefore, adapting does not mean that all moorings go. Principle also allows for debate with others who have other principles, and thus it enlarges the number of options.

The public church as a constituent in the public community of communities shares traditions, reason, aspects of Enlightenment, civic purpose, and transecting philosophies with many of the constituents and collegia in the larger civic order. It also exemplifies and makes room for internal variety, including in its distinctives, Christian theology. But as a whole this churchly cluster brings from its grasp of revelation many elements of use in public discourse.

Thus in response to its affirmation of God the creator are special motives, particular sanctions for what the good person or community would do on the basis of other motives. The sign of the New Creation provides many of these. As a church, it should be especially responsive to the notion of community. As a hearer of the word of God, including the law which comes uncompromisingly, this churchly cluster should move into the larger community with a special regard for the majesty of "the law beyond the laws." As a community in time, the church will be especially careful about tradition. Tinged with a prophetic reminiscence, which is a timid way of saying that it is to listen to the word of judgment on itself, this community should be capable of self-revision and reform.

As for the core of its witness, the church most of all insists on responsibility to the God beyond the gods. It is to be an agent of care for the neighbor and of carefulness about detail. All this it claims without knowing anything about a monopoly on knowledge or discernment.

The church has a special investment of care in these fields because of its long history of involvement with law, medicine, and barter. When it yielded monopoly, which means when it ceased to be the privileged informer of the disciplines and guilds, many of its leaders were confused by the secular agencies that displaced it. Mutual hostility developed. "We pass each other in the hall," said a surgeon friend when asked about a chaplain who had national renown for expertise in medical ethics and in the theological understanding of healing. Curricula on ethics in professional fields give assent to the idea of courses on ethics and moral contexts but these are often taught perfunctorily. A typical theological library may have shelves full of books on ethics and war, industry, labor, medicine, race, and sex. There will only be one or two on ethics and business, though most congregations in middle-class America, whether among black churches or white or racially mixed ones, are likely to have a significant number of business and professional members. "The dialogue between church and business has broken off," say some, who would be hard put to prove when it ever started.

To some it may seem evasive or distracting to devote these pages on public church ethics to the professions in America. The church thus constituted may be so muted, so immobilized that it will grow unsympathethic with Christians who must seek liberation from overt oppression. Advocates of some forms of liberation theology may find this approach too domestic and tame, too unresponsive to the prophetic. But the illustration comes with good grace. First, it is likely that liberation theologies, whether for women, blacks, people in poverty, or residents of the southern hemisphere, will get whatever hearing they do only in the public church. The conservative, fundamentalist, privatist, and sectarian clusters will give it no hearing at all. Second, if it is the case that the majority in American society do not regard theirs as a prerevolutionary society, they do well to handle in the light the kind of ethical issues that are before them, that can make a difference now.

In this conception, most congregations and communities in the public church can become communities of listeners, to start the conversation. In rural communities, farmers today have expertise and interests that are often overlooked in technological and governmental centers. A middle-size parish more likely than any other community institution brings professionals together from various fields over more sustained bases and on deeper levels of intimacy than other organizations. Many ethical problems should inspire a community address, but there are few provisions in secular America for airing them with people of other professions and with people who make up the clienteles or the groups that can make a difference in the lives of those who have no voice. This is a field in which bibliographies are growing, resources are becoming more available, and there is beginning to be a fund of expertise to use for inaugurating inquiries.

The end of such ethical exploring in public church components is not an agreement or a mandate to impose the Christian answer on pluralist America. After confrontation, it may be that two or more voices emerge from the conversation. But they will have heard each other as they now do not. Clinical, legal, commercial, consumer, and theological languages will come together. People learn the problems of the professions and interests better when someone they know voices them, than when they come from a distance.

Theological assumptions animate the probes. Participants in the public church believe that God the creator and preserver is in the grand design and the details of vocation and decision. God has provided mandates and calls for responsibility in a broken world. The Lord of the church has established a community of acceptance and care for the overcoming of distance born of disagreements and failures. The public church and its subcommunities will not have and should not seek to claim the whole domain for themselves. But they have a special calling to speak up for the Word they hear among the people who live by their story and, through them, speak to the larger community.

Conclusion: Prospects

The public church will share the difficulties of all other kinds of institutional religion in the decades to come. The crisis of legitimacy that affects organizations will limit it. The burdens of inflation will force on its leaders concerns for self-perpetuation which can inhibit its mission. Religious forces that take easier ways by making totalist or tribalist claims or by catering to private interest will have an advantage over the public church if it accepts its agenda of complexity. Most people will consider the combination of "special interiority" and "specific openness" to be an expensive and even foolish vision. The combination of commitment and civility looks psychologically improbable. Yet there are some resources to sustain such a community of communities in the decades ahead.

The components of the public church have learned to rely on a sense of vocation, not a dream of progress. Mainline Protestants and some of the Catholics, particularly those influenced by Teilhard de Chardin, sometimes have acted as if the reason for them to fulfill their calling was that success must follow. What Paul Tillich called a hidden utopianism or metaphysics of progress colored their acts. If one could not transform the world into the image of Christ or the Kingdom of God, what value was there in churchly endeavor?

Twentieth-century events have repeatedly dashed the hopes of those who preached the Social Gospel, Omega Point, or the Secular City. But here another side of the public church makes its witness. The evangelicals have been less ready to see history turn out well, perhaps because among the millennialists the world-pessimists won out over the progressives. Many of them are faithful to some biblical prophecies of worse times ahead, but still affirm the validity of temporal life. Catholicism also has another side which does not rely on

167

things getting better in order to encourage the church to be doing better. These two constituencies can guide mainline Protestants to help them reach for other resources in their idea of the calling. In the Christian scheme each day has intrinsic worth. Believers participate not for the sake of what their work does toward tomorrow, but because they are forgiven, made free to accept what God gives as tasks in any day.

The interplay of these forces can inspire the public church to intervene in history despite its realism. Its evangelicals were virtuosos at preaching about the depth of original sin and the variety of actual sins. This preaching often led them to be paralyzed about human possibility. Here the mainline and the Catholics step in and draw on their resources. The story of human limits was a way to glorify God and portray human need, not to numb human agents. So Christianity that stresses the incarnation balances that which concentrates on the atonement. The human is the race for which Jesus Christ had to die. But this is also the race in which he chose to live, the race he honored by participation. This is a race that lives not only by the sign of fallen Adam but also by the risen Christ. One does not need to conjure a philosophy of self-esteem or teach Christians to become little engines that could. The faith teaches them a sense of "self-presence" and points to their created, derived, and restored worth.

Third, the public church does not need to rely on a world that is, in Albert Cleage's term, "religiocified." Originally it was the Constantinian Catholic that taught and brought to America the notion that the public order had to be under Christian dominion. Then the mainline picked it up while imperial Protestantism tried to forge a Christian civilization in the nineteenth century. Now it is the more militant evangelicals and some of their kin in the public church who are tempted to reach for the language of Christianization. Out of it have come the injunctions to "win the continent for Christ," or "declare that America lives by the law of Christ." People are commended to elect only Born Again Christians, and then all will be well.

The public church tempers this claim by reaching for different resources in Augustine, Calvin, Luther, and others who preached a *justitia civilis*, a civil righteousness. This meant that God was active producing good through people who do not know God. An approach of this sort relies on the distinction between what we have called saving faith and constituting faith. The temptation remains to advance religion as religion over the secular reality. When the Vatican secretariat for nonbelievers looks around and finds few nonbelievers and more other-believers, some Catholic apologists and strategists lean forward. Their work seems half done. They feel at home, hoping to do business with religion, which means with half-Christianized humanity. But the Bible that knows of the Persian ruler Cyrus as a shepherd of Yahweh's people allows for powers that seem far from being religious or, in this case, from being Christian as "ordained of God."

The public church, because of its interactions, is more likely than are its churches in isolation, to proclaim the intrinsic values of grace and hope. In their competitions they may tend to be very busy and programmatic as they keep up appearances and measure performance by statistics. When they let down barriers of defensiveness and look at what is achieved among them, they are more likely to see that each day is a gift. Catholic theologian Monika Hellwig once alerted us, during the prime years of the theology of hope, that no such theology makes sense unless it gains resonances in the homes for the aged or in the wards of the terminally ill. People there are living in a hope that is not dependent upon public action but upon the promise of God that love is stronger than death, and that nothing shall separate believers from the love of God in Christ Jesus.

This grace allows for the tilting of believers' hearts ever so subtly from despair to hope, a tilt that José Ortega y Gasset described as more decisive than any history made by war, earthquake, or cataclysm. They are going to need that hope. Near the end of the second millennium one cannot point to many signs that promise survival of religions that are not belligerent, tribes that do not turn tribal. We may also expect new assertiveness from the secular order, which has given a free ride to the religious forces during the period when technology failed. But latent hostility on its part remains. Too much religion has turned out to be unaccountable, grasping, or full of scandal, and in all three such cases it will evoke counter-religious reaction. The militant religionists will use the reaction further to undercut forces of empathy in the name of a Christianity that takes risks.

The choices are stark: a bleakly secular landscape or a belligerently religious one or, more likely, a continued mix of both. Over against them, however, we can compile some assets. Countless congregations in the public church *do* work effectively. They are well led by clergy and laity who do not look back to good old days. The ecumenical spirit has outlived the older forms of the movement, enough to make our picture of the public church plausible. We have been reporting news of existence and emergences, not merely wishing that something could begin to exist. The growth of Christianity in the southern hemisphere brings a new drama to Christian life, thanks to the struggles for liberation in South America and the wildly diverse forms of the faith in Africa.

We have noted other positive turns in the road. Some believers have learned to adopt simple, reflective styles of living. A renewed sense that Christians must think, must even out-think someone, and not merely experience, is evident. The metaphor of the journey for the spiritual life has pulled people out of selfish security. The idea that the Christian story can animate people will make possible some reconceiving and remapping for that journey. Individual Christians are now less repressed about their body, their speech, their potential. Women, the aged, and people in minority groups have gained voices of a sort not heard in Christianity on such a wide scale before. Some of the young shame their elders by their faithfulness. The works of love live on, as congregations engage in activities of welfare and relief. Churches seek to recover the sense of the presence of God. Some in the belligerent churches have learned to see value in the lives of people who do not agree with them, and the wanly civil churches are learning to witness again.

Taken together, these are signs that many Christian people have not chosen to jump ship. They have not known what is in the night if they jump, and they recognize that their ship may be fogbound, not sinking. They have learned to choose their attitudes in the face of every possible circumstance. They will have to call forth more and more their reliance on their Christic center if they want to continue to live exposed, without thick boundaries against the world. If so, this communion of communions, this family of apostolic churches, will play its modest part in holding back the darkness. Its "specific openness" bids it to be faithful and intelligent, to pick its shots well in the face of the *res publica*, the public prospect.